An Introduction to
COMBINATORY ANALYSIS

MAXWELL PRESS

An Introduction to
COMBINATORY ANALYSIS

P.A. Macmahon

D.Sc., Sc.D, LL.D., F.R.S

Member of the St. John's College,
Cambridge

MAXWELL PRESS

Chennai   Trichy   New Delhi

MAXWELL PRESS

This edition has been published in india by arrangement with Carson Books, UK

ISBN 978-93-91270-62-9   Maxwell Press

All rights reserved   No. 44, Nallathambi Street,
Triplicane, Chennai 600 005

MJP 1154   © Publishers, 2022

Publisher :   C. Janarthanan

Publisher's Note

The legacy of a country is in its varied cultural heritage, historical literature, developments in the field of economy and science. The top nations in the world are competing in the field of science, economy and literature. This vast legacy has to be conserved and documented so that it can be bestowed to the future generation. The knowledge of this legacy is slowly getting perished in the present generation due to lack of documentation.

Keeping this in mind, the concern with retrospective acquiring of rare books has been accented recently by the burgeoning reprint industry. Maxwell Press is gratified to retrieve the rare collections with a view to bring back those books that were landmarks in their time.

In this effort, a series of rare books would be republished under the banner, "Maxwell Press". The books in the reprint series have been carefully selected for their contemporary usefulness as well as their historical importance within the intellectual. We reconstruct the book with slight enhancements made for better presentation, without affecting the contents of the original edition.

Most of the works selected for republishing covers a huge range of subjects, from history to anthropology. We believe this reprint edition will be a service to the numerous researchers and practitioners active in this fascinating field.

We allow readers to experience the wonder of peering into a scholarly work of the highest order and seminal significance.

Maxwell Press

PREFACE

THIS little book is intended to be an Introduction to the two volumes of *Combinatory Analysis* which were published by the Cambridge University Press in 1915–16. It has appeared to me to be necessary from the circumstance that some of my mathematical critics have found that the presentation of the general problem through the medium of the algebra of symmetric functions is difficult or troublesome reading. I was reminded that the great Euler wrote a famous algebra which was addressed to his man-servant, and had the object of anticipating and removing every conceivable difficulty and obscurity. Posterity gives the verdict that, in accomplishing this he was wonderfully successful.

From a general point of view it seems to me there is advantage on the one hand in explaining a complicated if not difficult matter to an untrained mind, and on the other in propounding a simple theory for the benefit of those who are highly trained. In this way certain vantage points may be reached which are not commonly attainable by the usual plan of addressing students in a style which is in proportion to their attainments. The advantage which has been spoken of accrues both to the writer and to the reader. The writer for example is likely to be led to points of view of whose existence he was previously unaware or aware of only sub-consciously. In attempting what is here proposed it is inevitable that much must be written that will appear to the reader to be self-evident and unworthy of statement. The intention is by a succession of such statements to arrive at facts which, by a quicker progression, would be difficult or troublesome to grasp. It is in analogy with a succession of likenesses of a person taken at small intervals of time such that little or no difference can be detected between any two successive pictures but between pictures taken at considerable intervals there is but a mere resemblance. The subject-matter of the book shews I believe that the algebra of symmetric functions and an important part of Combinatory Analysis are beautifully adapted to one another, and if I have succeeded in making that clear to the reader I shall be satisfied that the object of the book has been attained.

My grateful thanks are due to Professor J. E. A. Steggall, M.A. for much helpful criticism during the composition of the book.

P. A. M.

February, 1920.

TABLE OF CONTENTS

CHAPTER I

ELEMENTARY THEORY OF SYMMETRIC FUNCTIONS

CHAPTER II

OPENING OF THE THEORY OF DISTRIBUTIONS

CHAPTER III

DISTRIBUTION INTO DIFFERENT BOXES

CHAPTER IV

DISTRIBUTION WHEN OBJECTS AND BOXES ARE EQUAL IN NUMBER

CHAPTER V

DISTRIBUTIONS OF GIVEN SPECIFICATION

CHAPTER VI

THE MOST GENERAL CASE OF DISTRIBUTION

CHAPTER I

ELEMENTARY THEORY OF SYMMETRIC FUNCTIONS

1. A great part of Combinatory Analysis may be based upon the algebra of Symmetric Functions, and it is therefore necessary to have some clear definitions and simple properties of such functions before us.

An algebraic function of a number of numerical magnitudes is said to be Symmetrical if it be unaltered when *any* two of the magnitudes are interchanged. In algebra such magnitudes (or quantities) are denoted by letters of the alphabet.

Restricting ourselves to those functions which are rational it is clear, for example, that the simple sum of the quantities $a, \beta, \gamma, \ldots \nu$, n in number, is such a function. For the sum

$$a + \beta + \gamma + \ldots + \nu$$

is unaltered when any selected pair of the letters is interchanged. For this symmetric function, of which a is the type, we adopt the shorthand

$$\Sigma a.$$

Again, another symmetric function is

$$a^i + \beta^i + \gamma^i + \ldots + \nu^i,$$

because the enunciated conditions of symmetry are just as clearly satisfied as in the particular case $i = 1$.

We may denote this function by

$$\Sigma a^i,$$

the representative or typical term being alone put in evidence. This last expression includes all the integral symmetric functions, the representative term of which involves one only of the quantities. If we are not restricted to integral functions the representative term may be any rational function of a. For example

$$\Sigma \frac{a^s}{1 - a a^i} = \frac{a^s}{1 - a a^i} + \frac{\beta^s}{1 - a \beta^i} + \frac{\gamma^s}{1 - a \gamma^i} + \ldots + \frac{\nu^s}{1 - a \nu^i},$$

but we are, in most cases, concerned with the symmetric functions which are integral as well as rational.

M.

The function Σa^i is the sum of the ith powers of the quantities. It takes a leading part in the algebra of the functions.

The laws of this algebra do not depend upon the absolute magnitudes of the quantities a, β, γ, ... ν, so that usually it is not necessary to specify these quantities. Various notations have been adopted with the object of eliminating the actual magnitudes from consideration. Thus Σa^i is sometimes denoted by s_i; meaning thereby the sum of the ith powers of magnitudes which it is not needful to specify either in magnitude or (very often) in number. Others realising that in the algebra they have to deal entirely with the number i have denoted the same function by

$$(i),$$

viz. the number i in round brackets. This notation is of the greater importance because, as will become evident, it can be extended readily to rational and integral functions in general. Not only so; it is fundamentally important because it supplies the connecting link between the algebra of symmetric functions and theories which deal with numbers only and not with algebraic quantities.

2. Proceeding to functions whose representative terms involve two quantities, the simplest we find to be

$$a\beta + a\gamma + \beta\gamma + \ldots + \mu\nu,$$

which involves each of the $\frac{1}{2}n(n-1)$ combinations, two together, of the n quantities. It is visibly symmetrical.

This is denoted in conformity with the conventional notation by

$$\Sigma a\beta,$$

or by

$$(11),$$

the function being completely given when n is known.

Every function is considered to have a *weight*, which is equal to the sum of the numbers that, in the last notation, appear in the brackets.

Thus the functions (i), (11) have the weights i, 2 respectively.

When a number is repeated in brackets it is convenient to use repetitional exponents. Thus

(11) is frequently written in the form (1^2).

Of the weight one we have the single function

$$(1);$$

of the weight two, the two functions

$$(2),\ (1^2).$$

Observe that two functions present themselves because two objects can either be taken in one lot comprising both objects, or in two lots, one object in each lot. We express this by saying that the number 2 has two partitions. We have thus, of the weight two, a function corresponding to each partition of 2.

3. In the notation of the Theory of the Partition of Numbers the partitions of the number 2 are denoted by (2), (1^2). It is for this reason that the notation we are employing for symmetric functions is termed 'The Partition Notation.' Similarly in correspondence with the three partitions of 3, viz. (3), (21), (1^3), we have the symmetric functions

$$\Sigma a^3, \ \Sigma a^2 \beta, \ \Sigma a\beta\gamma$$

of the weight 3.

Of symmetric functions whose representative terms involve two of the n quantities we have the two types in which the repetitional exponents are alike, or different,

$$\Sigma a^i \beta^i \equiv a^i \beta^i + a^i \gamma^i + \beta^i \gamma^i + \ldots + \mu^i \nu^i = (i^2),$$

$$\Sigma a^i \beta^j \equiv a^i \beta^j + a^j \beta^i + \ldots + \mu^i \nu^j + \mu^j \nu^i = (ij),$$

involving $\tfrac{1}{2}n(n-1)$ and $n(n-1)$ terms respectively.

It is now an easy step to the function

$$\Sigma a_1^{i_1} a_2^{i_2} a_3^{i_3} \ldots a_s^{i_s},$$

wherein we have replaced the quantities $a, \beta, \gamma, \ldots \nu$ by the suffixed series $a_1, a_2, a_3, \ldots a_s$.

In the partition notation we write the function

$$(i_1 i_2 i_3 \ldots i_s),$$

where of course s cannot be greater than n.

It involves a number of terms which can be computed when we know the equalities that occur between the numbers $i_1, i_2, i_3, \ldots i_s$.

If we are thinking only of numbers, $(i_1 i_2 i_3 \ldots i_s)$ is a partition of a number $N = i_1 + i_2 + i_3 + \ldots + i_s$, and since a partition of N is defined to be any collection of positive integers whose sum is N we may consider the numbers $i_1, i_2, i_3, \ldots i_s$ to be in descending order of magnitude. These numbers are called the Parts of the partition and the partition is said to have s parts.

The series of functions denoted by (i) for different integer values of i constitute a first important set. They are sometimes called one-part functions.

4. A second important set is constituted by those functions which are denoted by partitions in which only unity appears as a part. It is

$$(1), \ (1^2), \ (1^3), \ \dots \ (1^n),$$

or $\qquad \Sigma a_1, \ \Sigma a_1 a_2, \ \Sigma a_1 a_2 a_3, \ \dots \ \Sigma a_1 a_2 a_3 \dots a_n.$

These are sometimes called unitary functions.

The set is particularly connected with the Theory of Algebraic Equations because

$$(x - a)(x - \beta)(x - \gamma) \dots (x - \nu)$$
$$= x^n - \Sigma a \cdot x^{n-1} + \Sigma a\beta \cdot x^{n-2} - \Sigma a\beta\gamma \cdot x^{n-3} + \dots,$$

the last term being $\pm \Sigma a\beta\gamma \dots \nu$, according as n is even or uneven. Hence considering the equation

$$x^n - a_1 x^{n-1} + a_2 x^{n-2} - a_3 x^{n-3} + \dots + (-)^n a_n = 0,$$

and supposing the n roots to be

$$a, \ \beta, \ \gamma, \ \dots \ \nu,$$

it is clear that

$$x^n - a_1 x^{n-1} + a_2 x^{n-2} - \dots + (-)^n a_n$$
$$= x^n - \Sigma a \cdot x^{n-1} + \Sigma a\beta \cdot x^{n-2} - \dots + (-)^n a\beta\gamma \dots \nu,$$

and we at once deduce the relations

$$a_1 = \Sigma a,$$
$$a_2 = \Sigma a\beta,$$
$$a_3 = \Sigma a\beta\gamma,$$
$$\dots\dots\dots\dots$$
$$a_n = a\beta\gamma \dots \nu.$$

These functions are frequently called 'elementary' symmetric functions because they arise in this simple manner.

It is sometimes convenient, undoubtedly, to regard the quantities $a, \ \beta, \ \gamma, \ \dots \ \nu$ as being the roots of an equation, the left-hand side of which involves the elementary functions with alternately positive and negative signs, but the notion is not essential to the study of the subject of symmetric functions.

5.   There is a third important series of functions.

Of the weight w there are functions which in the partition notation are denoted by partitions of the number w.

There is one function corresponding to every such partition.

Such a function, since it is denoted by a single partition, is called a Monomial Symmetric Function.

If we add all such functions which have the same weight we obtain, algebraically speaking, all the products w together of the quantities a, β, γ, ... ν, repetitions permissible.

Such a sum is called the Homogeneous Product-Sum of weight w of the n quantities.

It is usually denoted by h_w.

We have

$$h_1 = (1) = \Sigma a,$$
$$h_2 = (2) + (1^2) = \Sigma a^2 + \Sigma a\beta,$$
$$h_3 = (3) + (21) + (1^3) = \Sigma a^3 + \Sigma a^2\beta + \Sigma a\beta\gamma,$$

and so forth.

We have before us the three sets of functions

$$s_1, \ s_2, \ s_3, \ \ldots \ s_\nu, \ \ldots,$$
$$a_1, a_2, a_3, \ \ldots \ a_\nu,$$
$$h_1, h_2, h_3, \ \ldots \ h_\nu, \ \ldots$$

The first and third sets contain an infinite number of members, but the second set only involves n members where n is the number of the quantities a, β, γ, ...

6. The identity of Art. 4 which connects the functions $a_1, a_2, a_3, \ldots$

with a, β, γ, ... may be written, by putting $\dfrac{1}{y}$ for x,

$$1 - a_1 y + a_2 y^2 - \ldots + (-)^n a_n y^n \equiv (1 - ay)(1 - \beta y) \ldots (1 - \nu y),$$

or in the form

$$\frac{1}{1 - a_1 y + a_2 y^2 - \ldots + (-)^n a_n y^n} \equiv \frac{1}{(1 - ay)(1 - \beta y) \ldots (1 - \nu y)}$$

If we expand the last fraction in ascending powers of y, we obtain, in the first place,

$$+ (a + \beta + \gamma + \ldots + \nu)\, y$$
$$+ (a^2 + \beta^2 + \gamma^2 + \ldots + \nu^2 + a\beta + a\gamma + \beta\gamma + \ldots + \mu\nu)\, y^2$$
$$+ (a^3 + \beta^3 + \gamma^3 + \ldots + \nu^3 + a^2\beta + a\beta^2 + \ldots + \mu^2\nu + \mu\nu^2 + a\beta\gamma + a\beta\delta + \ldots + \lambda\mu\nu)\, y^3$$
$$+ \ldots.$$

It is clear that the coefficient of y^w is the homogeneous product-sum of weight w, so that we may write

$$\frac{1}{1 - a_1 y + a_2 y^2 - \ldots + (-)^n a_n y^n} \equiv 1 + h_1 y + h_2 y^2 + \ldots + h_w y^w + \ldots,$$

an identity.

Thence we obtain

$$\{1 - a_1 y + a_2 y^2 - \ldots + (-)^n a_n y^n\} (1 + h_1 y + h_2 y^2 + \ldots + h_w y^w + \ldots) = 1.$$

Since this is an identity we may multiply out the left-hand side and equate the coefficients of the successive powers of y to zero; obtaining

$$h_1 - a_1 = 0,$$
$$h_2 - a_1 h_1 + a_2 = 0,$$
$$h_3 - a_1 h_2 + a_2 h_1 - a_3 = 0,$$
$$\ldots\ldots\ldots\ldots\ldots\ldots\ldots\ldots\ldots$$
$$h_n - a_1 h_{n-1} + a_2 h_{n-2} - \ldots + (-)^n a_n = 0,$$
$$h_{n+1} - a_1 h_n + a_2 h_{n-1} - \ldots + (-)^n a_n h_1 = 0,$$
$$h_{n+2} - a_1 h_{n+1} + a_2 h_n - \ldots + (-)^n a_n h_2 = 0,$$
$$\ldots\ldots\ldots\ldots\ldots\ldots\ldots\ldots\ldots\ldots\ldots\ldots$$

relations which enable us to express any function h_w in terms of members of the series $a_1, a_2, a_3, \ldots a_n$.

7. In the applications to combinatory analysis it usually happens that we may regard n as being indefinitely great and then the relations are simply

$$h_1 - a_1 = 0,$$
$$h_2 - a_1 h_1 + a_2 = 0,$$
$$h_3 - a_1 h_2 + a_2 h_1 - a_3 = 0,$$
$$\ldots\ldots\ldots\ldots\ldots\ldots\ldots$$

continued indefinitely.

The before-written identity now becomes

$$(1 - a_1 y + a_2 y^2 - a_3 y^3 + \ldots ad\ inf.)(1 + h_1 y + h_2 y^2 + h_3 y^3 + \ldots ad\ inf.) \equiv 1,$$

and herein writing $-y$ for y and transposing the factors we find

$$(1 - h_1 y + h_2 y^2 - h_3 y^3 + \ldots ad\ inf.)(1 + a_1 y + a_2 y^2 + a_3 y^3 + \ldots ad\ inf.) \equiv 1,$$

an identity which is derivable from the former by interchange of the symbols a and h.

There is thus perfect symmetry between the symbols and it follows as a matter of course that in any relation connecting the quantities $a_1, a_2, a_3, \ldots$ with the quantities $h_1, h_2, h_3, \ldots$ we are at liberty to interchange the symbols a, h. This interesting fact can be at once verified in the case of the relations $h_1 - a_1 = 0$, etc.

Solving these equations we find

$$h_1 = a_1,$$
$$h_2 = a_1^2 - a_2,$$
$$h_3 = a_1^3 - 2a_1 a_2 + a_3,$$

and as shewn in works upon algebra

$$h_n = \Sigma \, (-)^{n+\pi_1+\pi_2+\dots+\pi_k} \frac{(\pi_1 + \pi_2 + \dots + \pi_k)!}{\pi_1! \, \pi_2! \dots \pi_k!} \, a_1{}^{\pi_1} a_2{}^{\pi_2} \dots a_k{}^{\pi_k},$$

where $\pi_1!$ denotes the factorial of π_1 and

$$\pi_1 + 2\pi_2 + 3\pi_3 + \dots + k\pi_k = n,$$

the summation being taken for all sets of positive integers $\pi_1, \pi_2, \dots \pi_k$ which satisfy this equation.

By interchange of symbols we pass to the relations

$$a_1 = h_1,$$
$$a_2 = h_1{}^2 - h_2,$$
$$a_3 = h_1{}^3 - 2h_1 h_2 + h_3,$$
$$\dots\dots\dots\dots\dots\dots\dots\dots$$
$$a_n = \Sigma \, (-)^{n+\pi_1+\pi_2+\dots+\pi_k} \frac{(\pi_1 + \pi_2 + \dots + \pi_k)!}{\pi_1! \, \pi_2! \dots \pi_k!} \, h_1{}^{\pi_1} h_2{}^{\pi_2} \dots h_k{}^{\pi_k}.$$

8. It is shewn in works upon algebra that the relations between the symbols $s_1, s_2, s_3, \dots$ and the symbols $a_1, a_2, a_3, \dots$ are

$$s_1 = a_1,$$
$$s_2 = a_1{}^2 - 2a_2,$$
$$s_3 = a_1{}^3 - 3a_1 a_2 + 3a_3,$$
$$\dots\dots\dots\dots\dots\dots\dots\dots$$
$$s_n = \Sigma \, (-)^{n+\pi_1+\pi_2+\dots+\pi_k} \frac{(\pi_1 + \pi_2 + \dots + \pi_k - 1)! \, n}{\pi_1! \, \pi_2! \dots \pi_k!} \, a_1{}^{\pi_1} a_2{}^{\pi_2} \dots a_k{}^{\pi_k}.$$
$$a_1 = s_1,$$
$$2! \, a_2 = s_1{}^2 - s_2,$$
$$3! \, a_3 = s_1{}^3 - 3s_1 s_2 + 2s_3,$$
$$\dots\dots\dots\dots\dots\dots\dots\dots$$
$$n! \, a_n = \Sigma \, (-)^{n+\pi_1+\pi_2+\dots+\pi_k} \frac{n!}{1^{\pi_1} . \, 2^{\pi_2} \dots k^{\pi_k} . \, \pi_1! \, \pi_2! \dots \pi_k!} \, s_1{}^{\pi_1} s_2{}^{\pi_2} \dots s_k{}^{\pi_k};$$

also between the symbols $s_1, s_2, s_3, \dots$ and $h_1, h_2, h_3, \dots$

$$s_1 = h_1,$$
$$s_2 = -(h_1{}^2 - 2h_2),$$
$$s_3 = h_1{}^3 - 3h_1 h_2 + 3h_3,$$
$$\dots\dots\dots\dots\dots\dots\dots\dots$$
$$s_n = \Sigma \, (-)^{\pi_1+\pi_2+\dots+\pi_k+1} \frac{(\pi_1 + \pi_2 + \dots + \pi_k - 1)! \, n}{\pi_1! \, \pi_2! \dots \pi_k!} \, h_1{}^{\pi_1} h_2{}^{\pi_2} \dots h_k{}^{\pi_k}.$$

$$h_1 = s_1,$$
$$2! \, h_2 = s_1{}^2 + s_2,$$
$$3! \, h_3 = s_1{}^3 + 3s_1 s_2 + 2s_3,$$
$$\dots\dots\dots\dots\dots\dots\dots\dots\dots$$
$$n! \, h_n = \Sigma \frac{n!}{1^{\pi_1} . 2^{\pi_2} \dots k^{\pi_k} . \pi_1! \, \pi_2! \dots \pi_k!} s_1{}^{\pi_1} s_2{}^{\pi_2} \dots s_k{}^{\pi_k}.$$

These are the principal properties of symmetric functions that will be of use.

9.   If we take any assemblage of letters such as $\alpha\alpha\beta\gamma$ and are not concerned with the order in which these letters are written, we have a 'Combination' of the letters. If however the order in which the letters are written be taken into account, we have a 'Permutation' of the letters. In the present case we have twelve permutations, viz.

$$
\begin{array}{cccccc}
\alpha\alpha\beta\gamma & \alpha\alpha\gamma\beta & \alpha\beta\alpha\gamma & \alpha\beta\gamma\alpha & \alpha\gamma\alpha\beta & \alpha\gamma\beta\alpha \\
\beta\alpha\alpha\gamma & \beta\alpha\gamma\alpha & \beta\gamma\alpha\alpha & \gamma\alpha\alpha\beta & \gamma\alpha\beta\alpha & \gamma\beta\alpha\alpha
\end{array}
$$

10.   In a similar manner if we take any collection of integers which add up to a given integer we have as above defined (Art. 3) a partition of the given number; here no account is taken of the order in which the parts of the partition may be written; but if order has to be taken into account each way of writing the parts is called a 'Composition' of the number, such composition appertaining to the particular partition which is involved. Thus of the number 9, $3321 \equiv 3^2 21$ is a partition which gives rise to the twelve compositions:

$$
\begin{array}{cccccc}
3321 & 3312 & 3231 & 3213 & 3132 & 3123 \\
2331 & 2313 & 2133 & 1332 & 1323 & 1233
\end{array}
$$

and it will be noticed that the compositions which appertain to the partition 3321 of the number 9 are in correspondence with the permutations of the combination $\alpha\alpha\beta\gamma$.

Moreover, in general the compositions which appertain to any given partition of a number are in correspondence with the permutations of a certain combination of letters.

11.   In pursuing the main object of this book, namely the study of the algebra of symmetric functions together with those theories of combination, permutation, arrangement, order and distribution which are summed up in the title 'Combinatory Analysis,' it is important to have some specific rules for arranging the order in which the terms of algebraic expressions are written down.

A monomial symmetric function, as defined in Art. 5, is the sum of a number of different combinations of the same type. In writing out at length these combinations of quantities a, β, ... ν we may adopt what is called the 'dictionary' (or alternatively 'alphabetical') order.

In any particular combination we write the a's first, then the β's, and so forth; also one combination is given priority of another if, considering the two combinations to be words, the dictionary would give the one word before the other.

This allusion to the dictionary, with which all persons are familiar, seems to define shortly and clearly the principle of order usually adopted. Thus we write the monomial function of four quantities a, β, γ, δ

$$\Sigma a^2 \beta \gamma$$

in the order
$$a^2\beta\gamma + a^2\beta\delta + a^2\gamma\delta + a\beta^2\gamma + a\beta^2\delta + a\beta\gamma^2$$
$$+ a\beta\delta^2 + a\gamma^2\delta + a\gamma\delta^2 + \beta^2\gamma\delta + \beta\gamma^2\delta + \beta\gamma\delta^2,$$

the dictionary order being in evidence both in each combination and in the order of the combinations.

Another order is sometimes useful. We may have, in each combination, the repetitional numbers always in the same order as they appear in the representative combination but *subject to this rule*, the letters in dictionary order.

The combinations thus written would then be arranged in dictionary order. Thus we might write

$$\Sigma a^2 \beta \gamma$$
$$= a^2\beta\gamma + a^2\beta\delta + a^2\gamma\delta + \beta^2 a\gamma + \beta^2 a\delta + \beta^2\gamma\delta$$
$$+ \gamma^2 a\beta + \gamma^2 a\delta + \gamma^2\beta\delta + \delta^2 a\beta + \delta^2 a\gamma + \delta^2\beta\gamma.$$

12. Again, frequently we have to write out at length the permutations of a given combination of letters. Here again it is usual to adopt the dictionary order, each permutation being regarded as a dictionary word. Thus the twelve permutations of $aa\beta\gamma$ are written

$$aa\beta\gamma \qquad aa\gamma\beta \qquad a\beta a\gamma \qquad a\beta\gamma a \qquad a\gamma a\beta \qquad a\gamma\beta a$$
$$\beta aa\gamma \qquad \beta a\gamma a \qquad \beta\gamma aa \qquad \gamma aa\beta \qquad \gamma a\beta a \qquad \gamma\beta aa.$$

13. When we have to write out symmetric functions, of the same weight, expressed in partition notation, we usually adopt numerical order, the meaning of which will be clear from the example

$$h_6$$
$$= (6) + (51) + (42) + (411) + (33) + (321) + (3111)$$
$$+ (222) + (2211) + (21111) + (111111),$$

where in each term the largest number available is written first, the next largest second, and so on; and in ordering the partitions numbers in descending order of magnitude are in the same relation as are the successive letters of the alphabet in dictionary order. The alternative method is to adopt the numerical order subject to the rule that the partitions are to be arranged in ascending order in regard to the *number of parts* involved.

This would give the expression

$$h_6$$
$$= (6) + (51) + (42) + (33) + (411) + (321) + (222)$$
$$+ (3111) + (2211) + (21111) + (111111).$$

When we have to write out the compositions associated with a given partition we adopt numerical order.

Thus associated with the partition (321) of the number 6 we have the compositions

$$(321), \ (312), \ (231), \ (213), \ (132), \ (123).$$

CHAPTER II

OPENING OF THE THEORY OF DISTRIBUTIONS

14. From the principles set forth in the concluding articles of Chapter I we can realise a definite way of expressing the result of algebraical multiplication.

Suppose that we have to form the product of a number of algebraical expressions each of which involves (say) three terms. The expressions are supposed to be given in a definite order from left to right. This order will be determined, usually, by the circumstances.

Let the factors be n in number, and, in the given definite order, denoted by

$$(a_1 + b_1 + c_1) (a_2 + b_2 + c_2) (a_3 + b_3 + c_3) \ldots$$
$$(a_{n-1} + b_{n-1} + c_{n-1}) (a_n + b_n + c_n),$$

where three terms are involved in each factor merely for the sake of simplicity.

To obtain a term of the product we select a term (any term) from each factor and place them in contact in the order in which they have been selected; the factors being dealt with in order from left to right. The term of the product, thus reached, may involve one, two or three of the symbols a, b, c according to the way that the selection is carried out. To place the terms (3^n in number) thus arrived at in a definite order we make our selections in such wise that the terms produced are in dictionary order. Thus the first three terms will be

$$a_1 a_2 a_3 \ldots a_{n-1} a_n,$$
$$a_1 a_2 a_3 \ldots a_{n-1} b_n,$$
$$a_1 a_2 a_3 \ldots a_{n-1} c_n,$$

and the last three

$$c_1 c_2 c_3 \ldots c_{n-1} a_n,$$
$$c_1 c_2 c_3 \ldots c_{n-1} b_n,$$
$$c_1 c_2 c_3 \ldots c_{n-1} c_n.$$

15. As an example, consider the development of $(\alpha + \beta)^n$. Writing down the n factors

$$(\alpha + \beta)(\alpha + \beta)(\alpha + \beta) \ldots (\alpha + \beta)(\alpha + \beta),$$

the multiplication, according to rule, gives for a few terms

$$a^n + a^{n-1}\beta + a^{n-2}\beta a + a^{n-2}\beta\beta + a^{n-3}\beta a a$$
$$+ a^{n-3}\beta a\beta + a^{n-3}\beta\beta a + a^{n-3}\beta\beta\beta + \ldots,$$

and the complete product for $n \doteq 4$ is

$$a^4 + a^3\beta + a^2\beta a + a^2\beta^2 + a\beta a^2 + a\beta a\beta + a\beta^2 a + a\beta^3$$
$$+ \beta a^3 + \beta a^2\beta + \beta a\beta a + \beta a\beta\beta + \beta\beta a a + \beta\beta a\beta + \beta\beta\beta a + \beta^4.$$

The combinations which appear are

$$a^4, \ \ a^3\beta, \ \ a^2\beta^2, \ \ a\beta^3, \ \ \beta^4,$$

and the product, as obtained by rule, involves all the permutations of these combinations, and no other terms.

The terms of the product are visibly in dictionary order and from the way in which the multiplication has been carried out each of the combinations necessarily appears as many times as it possesses permutations; so that when the terms are assembled so as to yield the formula of the binomial theorem

$$(a + \beta)^4 = a^4 + 4a^3\beta + 6a^2\beta^2 + 4a\beta^3 + \beta^4,$$

each numerical coefficient denotes the number of permutations of the combination of letters to which it is attached. The same remark can be made in regard to the general formula

$$(a + \beta)^n = a^n + \binom{n}{1} a^{n-1}\beta + \binom{n}{2} a^{n-2}\beta^2 + \ldots + \binom{n}{1} a\beta^{n-1} + \beta^n.$$

16. We proceed to another order of ideas by connecting the theory above sketched with a Distribution into different Boxes.

Suppose that we have four different (that is distinguishable) boxes A_1, A_2, A_3, A_4 arranged in order from left to right

A_1	A_2	A_3	A_4
a	a	β	β
a	β	a	β
a	β	β	a
β	β	a	β
β	a	β	a
β	a	a	a

and let us consider the selections of factor terms that were made in forming the product combination $a^2\beta^2$.

For the first selection we took the terms a, a, β, β from the first, second, third and fourth factors respectively. Place these letters in the four boxes A_1, A_2, A_3, A_4 respectively. Proceed in the same way for each of the six selections that produce the combination $a^2\beta^2$. We obtain the successive lines of letters shewn in the above scheme. We observe that we have distributed the four letters a, a, β, β into the four different boxes, one letter into each box, in every possible way, and that reading the lines of letters from left to right one such distribution corresponds to each permutation of the combination. From the mode of term selection, to form the product, each permutation must occur and there can be no other distributions into the boxes except those which correspond to the permutations.

We thus see that, if the binomial expression

$$(a + \beta)^n$$

be expanded, the coefficient of the term $a^m\beta^{n-m}$ is equal

(i)   to the number of permutations of the combination $a^m\beta^{n-m}$,

(ii)   to the number of ways in which the letters of the combination $a^m\beta^{n-m}$ can be distributed into n different boxes, one letter into each box.

17. By precisely the same argument we reach the conclusion that if the multinomial expression

$$(a_1 + a_2 + a_3 + \dots + a_n)^i$$

be expanded, the coefficient of the term

$$a_1{}^{i_1} a_2{}^{i_2} a_3{}^{i_3} \dots a_s{}^{i_s}$$

is equal

(i)   to the number of permutations of the combination $a_1{}^{i_1} a_2{}^{i_2} \dots a_s{}^{i_s}$,

(ii) to the number of ways in which the letters of the combination $a_1{}^{i_1} a_2{}^{i_2} \dots a_s{}^{i_s}$ can be distributed into i different boxes, so that each box contains one letter.

We now remark that since $a_1 + a_2 + a_3 + \dots + a_n$ is a symmetric function of the n quantities, the expression

$$(a_1 + a_2 + a_3 + \dots + a_n)^i$$

is also a symmetric function. Hence every term of the expansion which is also a term of the function

$$\Sigma a_1{}^{i_1} a_2{}^{i_2} a_3{}^{i_3} \dots a_s{}^{i_s} \equiv (i_1 i_2 i_3 \dots i_s)$$

must appear with the same coefficient.

Hence we may say that when

$$(a_1 + a_2 + a_3 + \dots + a_n)^i$$

is expanded the coefficient of symmetric function

$$\Sigma a_1{}^{i_1} a_2{}^{i_2} \dots a_s{}^{i_s}$$

is equal

(i) to the number of permutations of the combination $a_1^{i_1} a_2^{i_2} \ldots a_s^{i_s}$,

(ii) to the number of ways in which the letters of the combination $a_1^{i_1} a_2^{i_2} \ldots a_s^{i_s}$ can be distributed into i different boxes, one letter into each box.

18. We have spoken of the distribution of letters into boxes. The letters may represent objects or things and it is often more convenient to speak of the distribution of objects rather than of letters. The objects are sufficiently specified by the repetitional numbers $i_1, i_2, \ldots i_s$. We can therefore properly define the objects distributed or permuted by saying that they have a Specification

$$(i_1 i_2 \ldots i_s)$$

which is necessarily some partition of i, the whole number of objects.

Also the number of ways in which the distribution into boxes can take place depends upon the identities that may exist between them. The boxes being such that there are no identities—in fact representable by

$$A_1, A_2, \ldots A_i,$$

we have only to regard the repetitional numbers, which in this case consist of i units. The Box Specification is therefore

$$(1^i),$$

and the distribution which we have had under view may be described as of objects specified by $(i_1 i_2 i_3 \ldots i_s)$ into boxes specified by (1^i), where

$$i_1 + i_2 + i_3 + \ldots + i_s = i.$$

19. The actual number of permutations or distributions is readily obtained. If the objects be all different, or in other words of specification (1^i), we may select an object for box A_1 in i ways; from the $i-1$ remaining objects we can select our object for box A_2 in $i-1$ ways; consequently we can use the boxes A_1, A_2 in $i(i-1)$ ways; similarly we can use the boxes A_1, A_2, A_3 in $i(i-1)(i-2)$ ways, and the whole of the boxes in $i(i-1)(i-2) \ldots 2 \cdot 1$ or in $i!$ ways. Hence there are $i!$ ways of distributing objects of specification (1^i) into boxes of specification (1^i). Now suppose i_1 of the objects are identical. In any distribution certain boxes i_1 in number will contain the same objects and if we now replace these similar objects by different objects we find that we can do this in $i_1!$ ways corresponding to i_1 permutations of the i_1 different objects. Hence the former distributions are $i_1!$ times as numerous as the latter, and therefore we find that the latter distributions can take place in

$$\frac{i!}{i_1!} \text{ ways.}$$

Similarly if other i_2 objects be identical the number of distributions is

$$\frac{i!}{i_1!\,i_2!},$$

and finally if the specification of the objects be

$$(i_1\,i_2\,\ldots\,i_s)$$

the number of distributions into boxes of specification (1^i) is

$$\frac{i!}{i_1!\,i_2!\,\ldots\,i_s!}.$$

This number therefore enumerates the permutations of objects of specification $(i_1\,i_2\,\ldots\,i_s)$.

20. In the partition notation the multinomial theorem may be written

$$(1)^i = \Sigma\,\frac{i!}{i_1!\,i_2!\,\ldots\,i_s!}\,(i_1\,i_2\,\ldots\,i_s),$$

the summation being for every partition of the number i.

It will be observed that the multinomial theorem involves the enumeration of the permutations of all combinations of letters that it is possible to form. For this reason it is often said to be the 'Generating Function' for the enumeration of permutations. Since it also enumerates certain distributions it may be said to be the 'Distribution Function' for the distribution of objects into boxes of specification (1^i), one object being placed in each box.

21. From this first very elementary case of distribution we can at once derive an interesting corollary.

Suppose that we have to distribute i objects into $i+j$ different boxes, so that the box specification is (1^{i+j}) subject to the condition that no box is to contain more than one object. It is clear that in any distribution there must be j empty boxes, and that we may place in each of them one of j new and identical objects.

These j new objects have the specification (j). Hence the problem before us is transformed into that of distributing objects of specification

$$(i_1\,i_2\,\ldots\,i_s\,j)$$

into boxes of specification (1^{i+j}).

The objects and boxes being now equi-numerous we have the case already considered and can see that the number of distributions is

$$\frac{(i+j)!}{i_1!\,i_2!\,\ldots\,i_s!\,j!}.$$

22. The reader will now observe that we can also pass from the latter to the former distribution, and that just as we can add any number to the specification of the objects in order to equalise the objects and boxes; so conversely, if we are given any specification of i objects and boxes of specification (1^i) we can cancel *any part* from the specification of the objects without altering the number of the distributions. Thus the distributions of objects $(i_1 i_2 \dots i_s)$ into boxes (1^i) are equi-numerous with the distributions of objects

$$(i_1 i_2 \dots i_{r-1} i_{r+1} \dots i_s)$$

into boxes (1^i). Here the number i_r is cancelled from the object specification, and r may be any of the numbers 1, 2, ... s.

As a simple example we find that objects of the specifications (21^2), (1^2), (21) have equi-numerous distributions into four different boxes, not more than one object in each box. These are

A_1	A_2	A_3	A_4
α	α	β	γ
α	α	γ	β
α	β	α	γ
α	β	γ	α
α	γ	α	β
α	γ	β	α

A_1	A_2	A_3	A_4
β	α	α	γ
β	α	γ	α
β	γ	α	α
γ	α	α	β
γ	α	β	α
γ	β	α	α

A_1	A_2	A_3	A_4
α	β		
α		β	
			β
	α	β	
	α		β
		α	β

A_1	A_2	A_3	A_4
β	α		
β			
β			α
	β	α	
	β		α
		β	α

A_1	A_2	A_3	A_4
α	α	β	
α	α		β
α	β	α	
α		α	β
α	β		α
α		β	α

A_1	A_2	A_3	A_4
β	α	α	
	α	α	β
β	α		α
	α	β	α
β		α	α
	β		

23. In the case of the binomial theorem another interpretation may be given to the coefficients.

Writing

$$(a + \beta)^n = \binom{n}{0} a^n + \binom{n}{1} a^{n-1}\beta + \ldots + \binom{n}{m} a^{n-m}\beta^m + \ldots + \binom{n}{n} \beta^n,$$

it has been shewn that the coefficient $\binom{n}{m}$ enumerates the permutations of the combination $a^{n-m}\beta^m$.

We can shew that the same number enumerates the number of ways of selecting m letters from an assemblage of n different letters. For consider the combination $a^3\beta^2$ and its ten permutations

$$\begin{array}{ccccc}
aaa\beta\beta & aa\beta a\beta & aa\beta\beta a & a\beta aa\beta & a\beta a\beta a \\
a\beta\beta aa & \beta aaa\beta & \beta aa\beta a & \beta a\beta aa & \beta\beta aaa
\end{array}$$

When an a is in the sth place from the left of the permutation substitute for it the suffixed a, a_s; thus obtaining, omitting the letters β entirely, the ten combinations

$$\begin{array}{ccccc}
a_1 a_2 a_3 & a_1 a_2 a_4 & a_1 a_2 a_5 & a_1 a_3 a_4 & a_1 a_3 a_5 \\
a_1 a_4 a_5 & a_2 a_3 a_4 & a_2 a_3 a_5 & a_2 a_4 a_5 & a_3 a_4 a_5
\end{array}$$

which constitute the ten combinations three together that can be formed from the letters of the combination $a_1 a_2 a_3 a_4 a_5$. If we had operated similarly with the letters β we would have reached the ten combinations two together that can be formed from the same combination of five letters, viz.

$$\begin{array}{ccccc}
a_4 a_5 & a_3 a_5 & a_3 a_4 & a_2 a_5 & a_2 a_4 \\
a_2 a_3 & a_1 a_5 & a_1 a_4 & a_1 a_3 & a_1 a_2
\end{array}$$

and we have no difficulty in realising that the number $\binom{n}{m} \equiv \binom{n}{n-m}$ enumerates the combinations m or $n - m$ together that can be formed from n different letters.

24. So far we have been concerned mainly with a distribution into different boxes, one object only being placed in each box. The results have been trivial, but they have supplied a connecting link between combinatory analysis and the algebra of symmetric functions. It will be shewn in what follows that this relationship can be greatly extended to the mutual advantage of combinatory analysis and the symmetrical algebra.

We proceed in the first place by removing the restriction that each box is to contain only one object. We consider distributions in which the number of boxes is less than the number of objects, so that some box or boxes must contain more than one object. We may join the issue in two ways. We may precisely define the distribution and then seek its connexion with the algebra; or we may set forth some combination of symmetric functions, which we can see will lead to a distribution of the required kind, and then seek to define the corresponding distribution. For the present we adopt the latter procedure and inquire into the development of the function

$$(1^2)^i \equiv (\Sigma a\beta)^i,$$

which for four quantities may be written

$$(a\beta + a\gamma + a\delta + \beta\gamma + \beta\delta + \gamma\delta)^i.$$

We carry out the multiplication of the i factors according to the process explained in Art. 14. The complete product is clearly a symmetric function, expressible as a linear function of monomials, of the weight $2i$, of the form

$$\Sigma a_1^{i_1} a_2^{i_2} \dots a_s^{i_s} \equiv (i_1 i_2 \dots i_s).$$

The monomial function just written will appear with a certain coefficient. What is the meaning of that coefficient in the theory of distributions?

In the process of multiplication we take any combination of two letters from the first factor with any combination from the second, and so on; until finally we take any combination from the ith factor and, assembling the letters thus obtained, we obtain, we suppose, a combination of letters

$$a_1^{i_1} a_2^{i_2} a_3^{i_3} \dots a_s^{i_s}.$$

Associated with this step in the multiplication we take i different boxes, that is to say of specification (1^i),

$$A_1 A_2 A_3 \dots A_i$$

corresponding to the i factors of the product in order from left to right and place the two-letter combinations which have been selected from the 1st, 2nd, ... ith factors in the boxes A_1, A_2, ... A_i respectively. We thus arrive at a distribution of the letters in $a_1^{i_1} a_2^{i_2} \dots a_s^{i_s}$ into i different boxes, subject to the sole condition that each box is to contain two different letters; or, as we may say, letters of specification (1^2). Making a similar distribution in correspondence with every selective step in the multiplication, which produces the combination $a_1^{i_1} a_2^{i_2} \dots a_s^{i_s}$, we reach a set of distributions which constitute the whole number of ways of distributing a definite set of objects of specification $(i_1 i_2 \dots i_s)$ into boxes of specification (1^i) in such wise that every box contains objects of specification (1^2). Since all the terms included in $\Sigma a_1{}^{i_1} a_2{}^{i_2} \ldots a_s{}^{i_s}$, regarded as denoting objects, have the same specification we say that the number of the distributions above defined is equal to the coefficient of symmetric function

$$(i_1 i_2 \ldots i_s)$$

in the development of the symmetric function ·

$$(1^2)^i.$$

Some examples supply simple verifications.

By ordinary multiplication we find that

$$(a\beta + a\gamma + a\delta + \beta\gamma + \beta\delta + \gamma\delta)^2 = \Sigma a^2\beta^2 + 2\Sigma a^2\beta\gamma + 6a\beta\gamma\delta,$$

or
$$(1^2)^2 = (2^2) + 2\,(21^2) + 6\,(1^4).$$

The distributions which give the three coefficients 1, 2, 6 are

A_1	A_2
$a\beta$	$a\beta$

A_1	A_2
$a\beta$	$a\gamma$
$a\gamma$	$a\beta$

A_1	A_2
$a\beta$	$\gamma\delta$
$a\gamma$	$\beta\delta$
$a\delta$	$\beta\gamma$
$\beta\gamma$	$a\delta$
$\beta\delta$	$a\gamma$
$\gamma\delta$	$a\beta$

Again, by developing
$$(\Sigma a\beta)^3 \equiv (1^2)^3$$

we find a term
$$15\Sigma a^2\beta^2\gamma\delta \equiv 15\,(2^2 1^2).$$

The fifteen distributions are

A_1	A_2	A_3
$a\beta$	$a\gamma$	$\beta\delta$
$a\beta$	$\beta\delta$	$a\gamma$
$a\gamma$	$a\beta$	$\beta\delta$
$a\gamma$	$\beta\delta$	$a\beta$
$\beta\delta$	$a\beta$	$a\gamma$
$\beta\delta$	$a\gamma$	$a\beta$

A_1	A_2	A_3
$a\beta$	$a\delta$	$\beta\gamma$
$a\beta$	$\beta\gamma$	$a\delta$
$a\delta$	$a\beta$	$\beta\gamma$
$a\delta$	$\beta\gamma$	$a\beta$
$\beta\gamma$	$a\beta$	$a\delta$
$\beta\gamma$	$a\delta$	$a\beta$

A_1	A_2	A_3
$a\beta$	$a\beta$	$\gamma\delta$
$a\beta$	$\gamma\delta$	$a\beta$
$\gamma\delta$	$a\beta$	$a\beta$

There is no simple expression for the general coefficient in the development of $(\Sigma a\beta)^i$; but when i is not too large there is a method of arriving at the value of any desired coefficient which will be given at a later stage.

25.　We pass on to consider the symmetric function product

$$(\Sigma a\beta)^i (\Sigma a)^j \equiv (1^2)^i (1)^j.$$

We write out the i factors followed by the j factors and proceed to obtain one term in the development by taking one combination of two letters from each of the first i factors and one letter from each of the last j factors. Assembling the letters so obtained we reach, suppose, a combination of $2i + j$ letters

$$a_1{}^{p_1} a_2{}^{p_2} \dots a_s{}^{p_s}.$$

In correspondence with the selective process that has resulted in this combination we take $i + j$ different, boxes, so that the box specification is (1^{i+j})

$$A_1 A_2 A_3 \dots A_i B_1 B_2 B_3 \dots B_j.$$

We place the two-letter combinations that were selected from the 1st, 2nd, ... ith factors in the boxes A_1, A_2, $\dots A_i$ respectively; and the single letters that were selected from the last j factors in the boxes B_1, B_2, ... B_j respectively. If we make a similar distribution for every case in which the selective process in the multiplication results in the combination $a_1{}^{p_1} a_2{}^{p_2} \dots a_s{}^{p_s}$ we will have obtained every distribution of a definite set of objects of specification $(p_1 p_2 \dots p_s)$ with boxes of specification (1^{i+j}) in such wise that in regard to i of the boxes A_1, A_2, $\dots A_i$ each box contains objects of specification (1^2), and in the remaining boxes B_1, B_2, ... B_j each box contains a single object. Hence we gather that distributions so specified are enumerated by the coefficient of the function $(p_1 p_2 \dots p_s)$ in the development of the product

$$(1^2)^i (1)^j.$$

In the distribution above defined the reader must notice that objects of specifications (1^2), (1) are restricted to the boxes A_1, A_2, ...; B_1, B_2, ... respectively. This implies that the boxes being in a definite order the $i + j$ combinations of objects are only allowed $i! j!$ permutations; that is to say that no exchange of combinations of objects of different specifications is allowed to take place. *If* such exchange be permitted $(i + j)!$ permutations between the combinations of objects may take place. The function that by its development enumerates the distributions must now be multiplied by

$$(i+j)! \div i! j! \equiv \binom{i+j}{i},$$

and we have the theorem :—

"If objects of specification $(p_1 p_2 \dots p_s)$ be distributed into boxes of specification (1^{i+j}) in such wise that i of the boxes (unspecified) receive objects of specification (1^2) and the remaining boxes objects of specification (1), the number of distributions is equal to the coefficient of the function $(p_1 p_2 \ldots p_s)$ in the development of the function

$$\binom{i+j}{i} (1^2)^i (1)^j.\text{"}$$

As an example it is found that

$$\binom{4}{2} (1^2)^2 (1)^2 = \ldots + 48\,(321) + \ldots.$$

The 48 distributions are

	A_1	A_2	A_3	A_4
the 12 permutations of	$\alpha\beta$	$\alpha\beta$	α	γ
24　　　　　„	$\alpha\beta$	$\alpha\gamma$	α	β
12　　　　　„	$\alpha\beta$	$\beta\gamma$	α	α

26. It is quite evident that the process by which we have reached this connecting link between distributions and the expansion of symmetric function products is of general application. The selective process is in correspondence with distribution when the factors of the symmetric function products are *any monomial symmetric functions whatever*.

For consider the product

$$(\Sigma a_1^{m_1} a_2^{m_2} \ldots a_t^{m_t})^i\, (\Sigma a_1^{n_1} a_2^{n_2} \ldots a_u^{n_u})^j \equiv (m_1 m_2 \ldots m_t)^i (n_1 n_2 \ldots n_u)^j.$$

We write out the i factors followed by the j factors and obtain one term in the development by taking one term from each of the $i+j$ factors. The i terms from the first i factors are each of them combinations of specification $(m_1 m_2 \ldots m_t)$. The j terms from the last j factors are each of them of specification $(n_1 n_2 \ldots n_u)$. The assemblage of $i+j$ terms is, suppose,

$$a_1^{p_1} a_2^{p_2} \ldots a_s^{p_s} \text{ of specification } (p_1 p_2 \ldots p_s).$$

In correspondence with the selective process we take $i+j$ boxes of specification (1^{i+j})

$$A_1 A_2 \ldots A_i \quad B_1 B_2 \ldots B_j.$$

We place the combinations that have been selected from the first i factors in the boxes A respectively and the remaining combinations in the boxes B.

If we make a similar distribution for every case in which the selective process results in the combination $a_1^{p_1} a_2^{p_2} \ldots a_s^{p_s}$ we will have obtained every distribution of a definite set of objects of specification $(p_1 p_2 \ldots p_s)$ into boxes of specification (1^{i+j}) subject to the condition that the combinations of specifications $(m_1 m_2 \dots m_t)$, $(n_1 n_2 \dots n_u)$ must be placed in the boxes A, B respectively.

Removing this condition we find as before a theorem :—

"If objects of specification $(p_1 p_2 \dots p_s)$ be distributed into boxes of specification (1^{i+j}) in such wise that i of the boxes (unspecified) receive objects of specification $(m_1 m_2 \dots m_t)$ and the remaining boxes objects of specification $(n_1 n_2 \dots n_u)$, the number of distributions is equal to the coefficient of the function $(p_1 p_2 \dots p_s)$ in the development of the function

$$\binom{i+j}{i} (m_1 m_2 \dots m_t)^i (n_1 n_2 \dots n_u)^j."$$

27. The same reasoning applies when any number of monomial symmetric functions are multiplied together and we may enunciate the general theorem :—

"If objects of specification $(p_1 p_2 \dots p_s)$ be distributed into boxes of specification $(1^{i+j+k+\dots})$ in such wise that i unspecified boxes receive objects of specification $(m_1 m_2 \dots m_t)$, j other unspecified boxes objects of specification $(n_1 n_2 \dots n_u)$, k other unspecified boxes objects of specification $(o_1 o_2 \dots o_v)$, etc., the number of distributions is equal to the coefficient of the function $(p_1 p_2 \dots p_s)$ in the development of the function

$$\frac{(i+j+k+\dots)!}{i!\,j!\,k!\dots} (m_1 m_2 \dots m_t)^i (n_1 n_2 \dots n_u)^j (o_1 o_2 \dots o_v)^k \dots."$$

Verifications may be made by means of the formula

$$(\Sigma a^2 \beta \gamma)(\Sigma a \beta \gamma) = \Sigma a^3 \beta^2 \gamma^2 + 2\Sigma a^3 \beta^2 \gamma \delta + 6\Sigma a^3 \beta \gamma \delta \epsilon$$
$$+ 3\Sigma a^2 \beta^2 \gamma^2 \delta + 6\Sigma a^2 \beta^2 \gamma \delta \epsilon + 10\Sigma a^2 \beta \gamma \delta \epsilon \theta,$$

otherwise written

$$(21^2)(1^3) = (32^2) + 2(321^2) + 6(31^4) + 3(2^31) + 6(2^21^3) + 10(21^5).$$

28. As it is important to be able to obtain readily the numerical values of such coefficients, we will subject this particular development to examination with the object of deducing general laws in the algebra of symmetric functions.

Suppose that the symmetric functions appertain to an unlimited number of quantities $a, \beta, \gamma, \dots$ and expand each side of the identity in powers of one of them, say a. The function (32^2) or $\Sigma a^3 \beta^2 \gamma^2$ involves some terms which do not contain a; terms such as $\beta^3 \gamma^2 \delta^2$ for example. The aggregate of these terms is (32^2) regarded as appertaining to the set of quantities $\beta, \gamma, \delta, \dots$, the original set with the omission of a. The function involves no terms containing the first power of a, but it has terms such as $a^2 \beta^3 \gamma^2$ which contain the second power of a, the aggregate of which is $a^2 (32)$, if (32) now appertains to the set $\beta,\ \gamma,\ \delta,\ \ldots$. Lastly it involves terms $a^3 (2^2)$, where (2^2) refers to the set $\beta,\ \gamma,\ \delta,\ \ldots$.

Hence we may write

$$(32^2) = (32^2)' + a^2 (32)' + a^3 (2^2)',$$

the dashed round bracket denoting that the symmetric functions refer to the deficient set of quantities $\beta,\ \gamma,\ \delta,\ \ldots$.

Similarly

$$(321^2) = (321^2)' + a (321)' + a^2 (31^2)' + a^3 (21^2)',$$
$$(31^4) = (31^4)' + a (31^3)' + a^3 (1^4)',$$
$$(2^31) = (2^31)' + a (2^3)' + a^2 (2^21)',$$
$$(2^21^3) = (2^21^3)' + a (2^21^2)' + a^2 (21^3)',$$
$$(21^5) = (21^5)' + a (21^4)' + a^2 (1^5)'.$$

The right-hand side of the identity may therefore be written

$$(32^2)' + 2 (321^2)' + 6 (31^4)' + 3 (2^31)' + 6 (2^21^3)' + 10 (21^5)'$$
$$+ a \{2 (321)' + 6 (31^3)' + 3 (2^3)' + 6 (2^21^2)' + 10 (21^4)'\}$$
$$+ a^2 \{(32)' + 2 (31^2)' + 3 (2^21)' + 6 (21^3)' + 10 (1^5)'\}$$
$$+ a^3 \{(2^2)' + 2 (21^2)' + 6 (1^4)'\}.$$

As regards the left-hand side, since

$$(21^2) = (21^2)' + a (21)' + a^2 (1^2)',$$
$$(1^3) = (1^3)' + a (1^2)',$$

we find that

$$(21^2) (1^3) = (21^2)' (1^3)' + a \{(21)' (1^3)' + (21^2)' (1^2)'\}$$
$$+ a^2 \{(1^2)' (1^3)' + (21)' (1^2)'\} + a^3 (1^2)' (1^2)'.$$

Now equating the coefficients of like powers of a (omitting the ease a^0) and suppressing the dashes to the round brackets by converting the set of quantities $\beta,\ \gamma,\ \delta, \ldots$ into the set $a,\ \beta,\ \gamma, \ldots$ through writing $a,\ \beta,\ \gamma, \ldots$ for $\beta,\ \gamma,\ \delta, \ldots$ respectively, we obtain the derived formulae

$$(21) (1^3) + (21^2) (1^2) = 2 (321) + 6 (31^3) + 3 (2^3) + 6 (2^21^2) + 10 (21^4),$$
$$(1^2) (1^3) + (21) (1^2) = (32) + 2 (31^2) + 3 (2^21) + 6 (21^3) + 10 (1^5),$$
$$(1^2)^2 = (2^2) + 2 (21^2) + 6 (1^4).$$

Thus we can derive, from any given identity, a number of other identities of lower weights. The very simple process is that of expansion in ascending powers of the quantity a.

We observe that the coefficient of a^m in any monomial function is obtained by merely deleting the part m from the partition which denotes the function; if the part m be not present the coefficient is zero. Observe also that in the product $(21^2) (1^3)$ the highest power of a that presents itself is 3 because 2, 1 are the largest parts in the factors respectively and $2 + 1 = 3$. It follows at once that the coefficient of a^3 in the product is found by simply obliterating the first or largest part in each factor. We thus arrive at the coefficient $(1^2)^2$. Thus from the original identity

$$(21^2)(1^3) = (32^2) + 2(321^2) + 6(31^4) + \text{ other terms which involve no part,}$$

in the partitions, as large as 3, we derive, at sight, the new identity

$$(1^2)^2 = (2^2) + 2(21^2) + 6(1^4).$$

From this we discover immediately new theorems in distribution. As an example, since

$$2(21^2)(1^3) = \ldots + 12(31^4) + \ldots,$$
$$(1^2)^2 = \ldots + 6(1^4) + \ldots,$$

we can assert that the number of distributions of objects of specification (31^4) into boxes of specification (1^2) in such wise that the boxes contain objects of specification (21^2) and (1^3) is twice the number of distributions of objects of specification (1^4) into boxes of specification (1^2) in such wise that both boxes contain objects of specification (1^2).

Examination of the distributions verifies this conclusion and the theory we are now discussing might have been entirely based upon a study of the distributions.

29. In order to facilitate the process of taking the coefficients of a^m in a symmetric function it is convenient to adopt a mathematical short-hand. Let the symbol

$$D_m,$$

placed before any symmetric function, stand for the phrase
'the coefficients of a^m in.'
Then when D_m is prefixed to a monomial function expressed in the partition notation, the result is the deletion of the part m from the partition; if the part m be not present the result is zero; if m itself be zero the result is to leave the function unaltered or, as we may say, to multiply the function by unity. For example

$$D_3(32^2) = (2^2); \quad D_2(32^2) = (32); \quad D_3(3) = 1;$$
$$D_4(32^2) = D_1(32^2) = 0; \quad D_0(32^2) = (32^2)*.$$

* It should be stated that the reader who is acquainted with the differential calculus will realise that D_m is effectively a partial differential operator of the order m which is expressible by means of symmetric functions in a variety of ways and, in particular, in terms of the elementary functions (1), (1^2), (1^3), ... which have been denoted above also by a_1, a_2, a_3, ... It was brought to light in 1883, *Proc. Lond. Math. Soc.*, by James Hammond and is freely used in 'Combinatory Analysis' and in many researches by the author which have been published in Scientific Journals during the past thirty years. The methods of the calculus are not necessary for this elementary exposition and the requisite properties of the symbol will be set forth without its aid.

30. Any symmetric function F may be written in ascending powers of the quantity a in the form

$$D_0 F + a D_1 F + a^2 D_2 F + \ldots,$$

in accordance with the definition of $D_m F$.

Hence the product of two functions F_1, F_2 is

$$(D_0 F_1 + a D_1 F_1 + a^2 D_2 F_1 + \ldots)(D_0 F_2 + a D_1 F_2 + a^2 D_2 F_2 + \ldots),$$

or
$$\begin{aligned}
&D_0 F_1 D_0 F_2 \\
&+ a\ (D_0 F_1 D_1 F_2 + D_1 F_1 D_0 F_2) \\
&+ a^2 (D_0 F_1 D_2 F_2 + D_1 F_1 D_1 F_2 + D_2 F_1 D_0 F_2) \\
&+ a^3 (D_0 F_1 D_3 F_2 + D_1 F_1 D_2 F_2 + D_2 F_1 D_1 F_2 + D_3 F_1 D_0 F_2) \\
&+ \ldots.
\end{aligned}$$

Moreover

$$F_1 F_2 = D_0 (F_1 F_2) + a D_1 (F_1 F_2) + a^2 D_2 (F_1 F_2) + \ldots.$$

Whence comparing the coefficients of a, a^2, a^3, $\ldots$,

$$\begin{aligned}
D_1 (F_1 F_2) &= D_0 F_1 . D_1 F_2 + D_1 F_1 . D_0 F_2, \\
D_2 (F_1 F_2) &= D_0 F_1 . D_2 F_2 + D_1 F_1 . D_1 F_2 + D_2 F_1 . D_0 F_2, \\
D_3 (F_1 F_2) &= D_0 F_1 . D_3 F_2 + D_1 F_1 . D_2 F_2 + D_2 F_1 . D_1 F_2 + D_3 F_1 . D_0 F_2,
\end{aligned}$$

$$\ldots \ldots \ldots \ldots \ldots \ldots \ldots \ldots \ldots \ldots \ldots \ldots \ldots \ldots \ldots \ldots \ldots$$

$$D_m (F_1 F_2) = \sum_{s=0}^{s=m} D_s F_1 . D_{m-s} F_2,$$

where on the right-hand side there is a term in correspondence with every composition (see Art. 10) of the number m, zero counting as a part. There are visibly $m + 1$ terms, but usually fewer than $m + 1$ will materialise because by the rules of operation many terms may vanish.

Similarly if we require the coefficients of a^m in the product of three functions

$$F_1 F_2 F_3,$$

the performance of the symbol D_m will involve a term

$$D_s F_1 . D_t F_2 . D_{m-s-t} F_3,$$

because one step in the multiplication is to find the coefficients of a^s, a^t, a^{m-s-t} in F_1, F_2, F_3 respectively, and then to multiply the three coefficients together.

Hence

$$D_m (F_1 F_2 F_3) = \sum_{s=0} \sum_{t=0} D_s F_1 . D_t F_2 . D_{m-s-t} F_3.$$

Since s, t, $m - s - t$ is a composition of the number into three parts, zero counting as a part, the symbol D_m breaks up into as many triads of symbols as the number m possesses compositions into three parts, zero counting as a part. The reader will have little difficulty in proving that the number of these compositions is

$$D_m\,(1 + a + a^2 + \ldots)^3 = D_m\,(1 - a)^{-3} = \binom{m + 2}{2} = \binom{m + 2}{m}.$$

In general, when the symbol D_m is prefixed to a product of i symmetric functions, it breaks up into as many i-ads of symbols as the number i possesses compositions into i parts, zero counting as a part. The number of such compositions is

$$D_m\,(1 - a)^{-i} = \binom{m + i - 1}{i - 1} = \binom{m + i - 1}{m}.$$

31. We can now see the importance of the study of the symbol, for evidently we can repeatedly operate with it, varying its suffix as may be desired, until a positive integer or zero is reached, and thus solve the problem of the multiplication of symmetric functions upon which the present view of combinatory analysis depends. For consider the product

$$(21^2)\,(1^3),$$

we have

$$D_3\,(21^2)\,(1^3) = D_2\,(21^2) \cdot D_1\,(1^3) = (1^2)\,(1^2),$$
$$D_3 D_2\,(21^2)\,(1^3) = D_2\,(1^2)\,(1^2) = D_1\,(1^2) \cdot D_1\,(1^2) = (1)\,(1),$$
$$D_3 D_2 D_1\,(21^2)\,(1^3) = D_0\,(1) \cdot D_1\,(1) + D_1\,(1) \cdot D_0\,(1) = 2\,(1),$$

and finally

$$D_3 D_2 D_1^2\,(21^2)\,(1^3) = 2 D_1\,(1) = 2.$$

Now we may write

$$(21^2)\,(1^3) = \ldots + C\,(321^2) + \ldots;$$

so that operating upon both sides with $D_3 D_2 D_1^2$ the right-hand side becomes C since every other term is reduced to zero by the operation. The calculation above shews that the left-hand side becomes 2 by the operation. Hence $C = 2$, and

$$(21^2)\,(1^3) = \ldots + 2\,(321^2) + \ldots.$$

We can in this way calculate the result of the product of any number of monomial functions and thus evaluate the number which enumerates a well-defined distribution of objects into boxes.

CHAPTER III

DISTRIBUTION INTO DIFFERENT BOXES

32. The theory set forth in the foregoing chapters enables us to make a great advance in combinatory analysis.

We are now able to attack the following problem.

Objects of any given specification are to be distributed into m different boxes, i.e. of specification (1^m); in how many ways can the distribution be made?

First consider the case of two boxes, denoted by A_1, A_2, and let the objects be w in number. It has been shewn in Art. 26 that if the specification of the objects be $(p_1 p_2 \ldots p_s)$ and the boxes are obliged to contain objects of specifications $(m_1 m_2 \ldots m_t)$, $(n_1 n_2 \ldots n_u)$, both specifications appearing, one in each box, the enumerating symmetric function product is $2 (m_1 m_2 \ldots m_t)(n_1 n_2 \ldots n_u)$ or $(m_1 m_2 \ldots m_t)^2$ if the partitions $(m_1 m_2 \ldots m_t)$, $(n_1 n_2 \ldots n_u)$ be identical.

We have merely to develop the product and seek the coefficient of the function $(p_1 p_2 \ldots p_s)$.

We now abolish the restriction and substitute another, viz. that the boxes are to receive, one of them w_1 objects and the other w_2 objects. We have

$$w_1 + w_2 = w \; ;$$

the w objects may have any specification and the w_1 and w_2 objects may have any specifications consistent with the condition that the assemblage of w_1 and w_2 objects must have the same specification as the w objects. If the specification of the w objects which are to be distributed be unknown the w_1 and w_2 objects may have specifications denoted by any partitions of w_1 and w_2 respectively. The w_1 objects may have therefore all specifications included in the function h_{w_1}, the w_2 objects all those included in the function h_{w_2}. If we form the functions

$$2 h_{w_1} h_{w_2} \text{ or } h_{w_1}^2,$$

according as w_1, w_2 are not or are equal, we obtain, upon multiplication, terms of the forms

$$2 (m_1 m_2 \ldots m_t) (n_1 n_2 \ldots n_u) \text{ or } (m_1 m_2 \ldots m_t)^2,$$

and it has been shewn already that these functions enumerate, on development, the distributions which are associated with the particular specifications $(m_1 m_2 \ldots m_t)$, $(n_1 n_2 \ldots n_u)$.

As an example let us distribute 4 objects into two different boxes so that one box, unspecified, contains 3 objects and the other box 1 object.

We have

$$2h_3 h_1 = 2\left\{(3) + (21) + (1^3)\right\}(1)$$
$$= 2\,(4) + 4\,(31) + 4\,(2^2) + 6\,(21^2) + 8\,(1^4),$$

leading to the conclusion that objects of specification (21^2) can be distributed in 6 ways and similarly when the objects have other specifications.

The distributions for all of the cases are:

Spec.	(4)		(31)		(2²)		(21²)		(1⁴)	
	A_1	A_2	A_1	A_2	A_1	A_2	A_1	A_2	A_1	A_2
	a^3	a	a^3	β	$a^2\beta$	β	$a\beta\gamma$	a	$a\beta\gamma$	δ
	a	a^3	β	a^3	β	$a^2\beta$	a	$a\beta\gamma$	δ	$a\beta\gamma$
			$a^2\beta$	a	$a\beta^2$	a	$a^2\beta$	γ	$a\beta\delta$	γ
			a	$a^2\beta$	a	$a\beta^2$	γ	$a^2\beta$	γ	$a\beta\delta$
							$a^2\gamma$	β	$a\gamma\delta$	β
							β	$a^2\gamma$	β	$a\gamma\delta$
									$\beta\gamma\delta$	a
									a	$\beta\gamma\delta$
No.	2		4		4		6		8	

in agreement with the theory.

33. Having thus obtained the enumerating function $2h_{w_1} h_{w_2}$ or $h_{w_1}^2$ for the special numbers w_1, w_2 we can include all cases by giving w_1, w_2 all possible values and adding the corresponding enumerating functions.

Thus for
$$w = 2 \text{ we have } h_1^2,$$
$$\text{,, } = 3 \quad \text{,,} \quad 2h_2 h_1,$$
$$\text{,, } = 4 \quad \text{,,} \quad h_2^2 + 2h_3 h_1,$$
$$\text{,, } = 5 \quad \text{,,} \quad 2h_3 h_2 + 2h_4 h_1,$$

and so on, while in general we seek the coefficient of x^w in the expansion of the function

$$(h_1 x + h_2 x^2 + h_3 x^3 + \ldots)^2.$$

We may state the theorem:—

"The number of distributions of objects of specification $(p_1 p_2 \ldots p_s)$ into boxes of specification (1^2) is equal to the coefficient of the function

$(p_1 p_2 \ldots p_s)$ in the development of the coefficient of x^w in the expansion of the function

$$(h_1 x + h_2 x^2 + h_3 x^3 + \ldots)^2$$

where $p_1 + p_2 + \ldots + p_s = w$."

As an example when $w = 4$,

$$2h_3 h_1 + h_2^2 = 3\,(4) + 6\,(31) + 7\,(2^2) + 10\,(21^2) + 14\,(1^4).$$

The distributions are

Spec.	(4)		(31)		(2^2)		(21^2)		(1^4)	
	A_1	A_2	A_1	A_2	A_1	A_2	A_1	A_2	A_1	A_2
	a^3	a	a^3	β	$a^2\beta$	β	$a^2\beta$	γ	$a\beta\gamma$	δ
	a^2	a^2	β	a^3	β	$a^2\beta$	γ	$a^2\beta$	δ	$a\beta\gamma$
	a	a^3	$a^2\beta$	a	$a\beta^2$	a	$a^2\gamma$	β	$a\beta\delta$	γ
			a	$a^2\beta$	a	$a\beta^2$	β	$a^2\gamma$	γ	$a\beta\delta$
			a^2	$a\beta$	a^2	β^2	$a\beta\gamma$	a	$a\gamma\delta$	β
			$a\beta$	a^2	β^2	a^2	a	$a\beta\gamma$	β	$a\gamma\delta$
					$a\beta$	$a\beta$	a^2	$\beta\gamma$	$\beta\gamma\delta$	a
							$\beta\gamma$	a^2	a	$\beta\gamma\delta$
							$a\beta$	$a\gamma$	$a\beta$	$\gamma\delta$
							$a\gamma$	$a\beta$	$\gamma\delta$	$a\beta$
									$a\gamma$	$\beta\delta$
									$\beta\delta$	$a\gamma$
									$a\delta$	$\beta\gamma$
									$\beta\gamma$	$a\delta$
No.	3		6		7		10		14	

34. Passing to the case of three boxes of specification (1^3) we consider a distribution in which the boxes contain w_1, w_2 and w_3 objects in any order respectively. The possible specifications of these lots of objects are shewn by the partitions of the functions which are terms in h_{w_1}, h_{w_2}, h_{w_3} and when these specifications are assigned the corresponding symmetric function products will be terms of the developed products

$$h_{w_1}^3, \quad 3h_{w_1}^2 h_{w_2}, \quad 6h_{w_1} h_{w_2} h_{w_3},$$

according to the equalities that present themselves in the numbers

$$w_1, \; w_2, \; w_3.$$

To see how this is we observe that from Art. 27 the distributions associated with specifications

$$(m_1 m_2 \ldots m_t), \; (n_1 n_2 \ldots n_u), \; (o_1 o_2 \ldots o_v)$$

are enumerated by the functions

$$(m_1 m_2 \ldots m_t)^3, \qquad 3 (m_1 m_2 \ldots m_t)^2 (n_1 n_2 \ldots n_u),$$
$$6 (m_1 m_2 \ldots m_t)(n_1 n_2 \ldots n_u)(o_1 o_2 \ldots o_v),$$

according to the identities that subsist between the three partitions. It is obvious that if $w_1 = w_2 = w_3$ the three partitions are all of the same weight and $h_{w_1}^{\,3}$ will give the three functions which have coefficients 1, 3, 6 respectively. If w_1, w_1, w_2 be the three weights $3h_{w_1}^{\,2} h_{w_2}$ involves on development the functions with coefficients 3, 6. Finally if w_1, w_2, w_3 are three different numbers, $6h_{w_1} h_{w_2} h_{w_3}$ produces all the functions which have the coefficient 6.

We can now include all cases by giving w_1, w_2, w_3 all values and adding the corresponding enumerating functions.

Thus for $\qquad w = 3$ we have $h_1^3,$

$$\begin{aligned}
&4 \quad\text{,,}\quad && 3h_2 h_1^2, \\
&5 \quad\text{,,}\quad && 3h_3 h_1^2 + 3h_1 h_2^2, \\
&6 \quad\text{,,}\quad && h_2^3 + 3h_4 h_1^2 + 6h_3 h_2 h_1,
\end{aligned}$$

and so on.

In general the enumerating h function is the coefficient of x^w in the expansion of

$$(h_1 x + h_2 x^2 + h_3 x^3 + \ldots)^3$$

and if we develop this h function the coefficient of the symmetric function $(p_1 p_2 \ldots p_s)$ is equal to the number of ways of distributing objects of specification $(p_1 p_2 \ldots p_s)$ into boxes of specification (1^3).

35.　We can now enunciate the *general* theorem :—

"The number of ways of distributing objects of specification $(p_1 p_2 \ldots p_s)$ into boxes of specification (1^m), no box being empty, is equal to the coefficient of

$$x^{p_1 + p_2 + \ldots + p_s} (p_1 p_2 \ldots p_s)$$

in the development of the function

$$(h_1 x + h_2 x^2 + h_3 x^3 + \ldots)^m.\text{"}$$

In order to be able to use this theorem in practice it is necessary to expand products of the functions $h_1, h_2, h_3, \ldots$ in terms of monomial functions. This may be readily accomplished by use of the operative symbols $D_0, D_1, D_2, \ldots$ because observing in the first place that

$$\begin{aligned}
D_0 h_3 &= D_0 \{(3) + (21) + (1^3)\} = (3) + (21) + (1^3) = h_3, \\
D_1 h_3 &= (2) + (1^2) = h_2, \\
D_2 h_3 &= (1) = h_1, \\
D_3 h_3 &= 1,
\end{aligned}$$

it is easy to see that

$$D_m h_w = h_{w-m}$$

is universally true if we agree that $h_0 = 1$.

If h_w' be the homogeneous product-sum, of weight w, of the quantities $\beta, \gamma, \delta, \ldots$ we may write

$$h_w = D_0 h_w' + a D_1 h_w' + a^2 D_2 h_w' + a^3 D_3 h_w' + \ldots,$$

so that

$$h_{w_1} h_{w_2} = (D_0 h_{w_1}' + a D_1 h_{w_1}' + a^2 D_2 h_{w_1}' + \ldots)(D_0 h_{w_2}' + a D_1 h_{w_2}' + a^2 D_2 h_{w_2}' + \ldots).$$

But

$$h_{w_1} h_{w_2} = D_0(h_{w_1}' h_{w_2}') + a D_1(h_{w_1}' h_{w_2}') + a^2 D_2(h_{w_1}' h_{w_2}') + \ldots.$$

Hence equating coefficients of like powers of a and suppressing the dashes by writing $a, \beta, \gamma, \ldots$ for $\beta, \gamma, \delta \ldots$

$$D_m(h_{w_1} h_{w_2}) = D_0 h_{w_1} . D_m h_{w_2} + D_1 h_{w_1} . D_{m-1} h_{w_2} + \ldots + D_m h_{w_1} . D_0 h_{w_2}$$
$$= h_{w_1} h_{w_2-m} + h_{w_1-1} h_{w_2-m+1} + \ldots + h_{w_1-m} h_{w_2},$$

shewing the way in which the symbol D_m operates upon any product $h_{w_1} h_{w_2}$. Compare Art. 30.

Similarly D_m operates upon a product of s functions $h_{w_1} h_{w_2} \ldots h_{w_s}$ through the medium of the various compositions of m into s parts, zero counting as a part.

36. Thus if we desire to develop the function

$$h_2^3 + 3h_4 h_1^2 + 6h_3 h_2 h_1$$

and require the coefficient of the function (51) the process may be as follows:

$$D_5 (h_2^3 + 3h_4 h_1^2 + 6h_3 h_2 h_1)$$
$$= D_2 h_2 . D_2 h_2 . D_1 h_2 + D_2 h_2 . D_1 h_2 . D_2 h_2 + D_1 h_2 . D_2 h_2 . D_2 h_2$$
$$+ 3 (D_4 h_4 . D_1 h_1 . D_0 h_1 + D_4 h_4 . D_0 h_1 . D_1 h_1 + D_3 h_4 . D_1 h_1 . D_1 h_1)$$
$$+ 6 (D_3 h_3 . D_2 h_2 . D_0 h_1 + D_3 h_3 . D_1 h_2 . D_1 h_1 + D_2 h_3 . D_2 h_2 . D_1 h_1)$$
$$= 3h_1 + 9h_1 + 18h_1 = 30h_1,$$

$$D_5 D_1 (h_2^3 + 3h_4 h_1^2 + 6h_3 h_2 h_1) = 30,$$

establishing that objects of specification (51) can be placed in boxes of specification (1^3), no box being empty, in 30 ways.

37. There is an alternative process which is of much interest.

Write $$h_1 x + h_2 x^2 + h_3 x^3 + \ldots = H,$$

and note that the coefficient of $x^{p_1+p_2+\ldots+p_s} (p_1 p_2 \ldots p_s)$ in H^m is

$$D_{p_1} D_{p_2} \ldots D_{p_s} \text{ (coefficient of } x^{p_1+p_2+\ldots+p_s} \text{ in } H^m).$$

Now $\quad H^m = (1 + H - 1)^m$

$$= (1 + H)^m - \binom{m}{1}(1 + H)^{m-1} + \binom{m}{2}(1 + H)^{m-2} - \ldots,$$

and $D_p(1 + H) = x^p(1 + H)$ by the law of operation.

Also $\quad D_p(1 + H)^2 = D_p(1 + H) . D_0(1 + H)$
$$+ D_{p-1}(1 + H) . D_1(1 + H) + \ldots,$$

there being one term on the right-hand side corresponding to every composition of p into two parts.

By Art. 30 the number of these compositions is

$$\binom{p + 1}{p} \equiv \binom{p + 1}{1}$$

Hence $\qquad x^{-p} D_p(1 + H)^2 = \binom{p + 1}{1}(1 + H)^2;$

also $\quad D_p(1 + H)^3 = D_p(1 + H) . D_0(1 + H) . D_0(1 + H) + \ldots$
$$+ D_a(1 + H) . D_b(1 + H) . D_c(1 + H)$$
$$+ \ldots,$$

there being one term on the right-hand side corresponding to each composition of p into three parts. The number of these compositions is, by Art. 30, $\binom{p + 2}{2}$.

We have $\qquad x^{-p} D_p(1 + H)^3 = \binom{p + 2}{2}(1 + H)^3,$

and generally $\qquad x^{-p} D_p(1 + H)^m = \binom{p + m - 1}{m - 1}(1 + H)^m.$

Making use of these results

$$x^{-p_1} D_{p_1} H^m = \binom{p_1 + m - 1}{m - 1}(1 + H)^m$$
$$- \binom{m}{1}\binom{p_1 + m - 2}{m - 2}(1 + H)^{m-1}$$
$$+ \binom{m}{2}\binom{p_1 + m - 3}{m - 3}(1 + H)^{m-2} + \ldots,$$

$$x^{-p_1 - p_2} D_{p_1} D_{p_2} H^m = \binom{p_1 + m - 1}{m - 1}\binom{p_2 + m - 1}{m - 1}(1 + H)^m$$
$$- \binom{m}{1}\binom{p_1 + m - 2}{m - 2}\binom{p_2 + m - 2}{m - 2}(1 + H)^{m-1}$$

and ultimately

$$x^{-p_1-p_2-\ldots-p_s} D_{p_1} D_{p_2} \ldots D_{p_s} H^m$$

$$= \binom{p_1+m-1}{m-1}\binom{p_2+m-1}{m-1}\ldots\binom{p_s+m-1}{m-1}$$

$$- \binom{m}{1}\binom{p_1+m-2}{m-2}\binom{p_2+m-2}{m-2}\ldots\binom{p_s+m-2}{m-2}$$

$$+ \binom{m}{2}\binom{p_1+m-3}{m-3}\binom{p_2+m-3}{m-3}\ldots\binom{p_s+m-3}{m-3}$$

$$- \ldots,$$

because we know that the right-hand side cannot involve x. We may therefore finally put x and therefore H equal to zero.

To verify the result of the preceding Article put

$$m = 3, \quad p_1 = 5, \quad p_2 = 1.$$

The formula gives

$$\binom{7}{2}\binom{3}{2} - 3\binom{6}{1}\binom{2}{1} + 3\binom{5}{0}\binom{1}{0}$$

$$= 63 - 36 + 3 = 30.$$

The series written down is thus established as enumerating the number of distributions of objects of specification $(p_1 p_2 \ldots p_s)$ into boxes of specification (1^m), no box being empty.

38. In the above investigation there is no restriction upon the number of times that any one of the quantities a, β, γ, ... may appear in the same box.

If no object is to appear more than once in the same box, a box which contains w_1 objects must contain objects denoted by the letters of one of the terms of $a_{w_1} \equiv (1^{w_1})$. Hence instead of the functions $h_1, h_2, h_3, \ldots$ we have presented to us the functions $a_1, a_2, a_3, \ldots$ and writing

$$a_1 x + a_2 x^2 + a_3 x^3 + \ldots = A$$

the enumerating function is the coefficient of $x^{p_1 + p_2 + \ldots + p_s}$ in

$$A^m.$$

If $m = 3$, the function which now enumerates the distributions into boxes of specification (1^3) is

$$a_2^3 + 3a_4 a_1^2 + 6a_3 a_2 a_1$$

$$\equiv (1^2)^3 + 3(1^4)(1^2)^2 + 6(1^3)(1^2)(1),$$

and if the objects be of specification (321) the number of distributions is

$$D_3 D_2 D_1 \{(1^2)^3 + 3(1^4)(1^2)^2 + 6(1^3)(1^2)(1)\}.$$

By the rule of operation we find

$$D_3 \{(1^2)^3 + 3\,(1^4)\,(1)^2 + 6\,(1^3)\,(1^2)\,(1)\}$$
$$= (1)^3 + 3\,(1^3) + 6\,(1^2)\,(1),$$

$D_3 D_2$ produces $\qquad\qquad 3\,(1) + 6\,(1),$

and finally $\quad D_3 D_2 D_1 \{(1^2)^3 + 3\,(1^4)\,(1)^2 + 6\,(1^3)\,(1^2)\,(1)\} = 9.$

The actual distributions are

A_1	A_2	A_3		A_1	A_2	A_3
$\alpha\beta\gamma$	$\alpha\beta$	α		$\alpha\beta$	$\alpha\beta$	$\alpha\gamma$
$\alpha\beta\gamma$	α	$\alpha\beta$		$\alpha\beta$	$\alpha\gamma$	$\alpha\beta$
$\alpha\beta$	$\alpha\beta\gamma$	α		$\alpha\gamma$	$\alpha\beta$	$\alpha\beta$
$\alpha\beta$	α	$\alpha\beta\gamma$				
α	$\alpha\beta\gamma$	$\alpha\beta$				
α	$\alpha\beta$	$\alpha\beta\gamma$				

39. In the alternative method we write

$$1 + A = 1 + a_1 x + a_2 x^2 + a_3 x^3 + \dots .$$

The reader will have no difficulty in establishing the formula

$$D_p\,(1 + A)^m = \binom{m}{p} x^p\,(1 + A)^m,$$

so that operating upon A^m in the form

$$(1 + A)^m - \binom{m}{1}(1 + A)^{m-1} + \binom{m}{2}(1 + A)^{m-2} - \dots$$

we readily reach the number which enumerates the distributions of objects of specification $(p_1 p_2 \dots p_s)$ into boxes of specification (1^m), no box being empty, subject to the condition that no particular object is to appear twice in the same box. The number is

$$\binom{m}{p_1}\binom{m}{p_2}\dots\binom{m}{p_s} - \binom{m}{1}\binom{m-1}{p_1}\binom{m-1}{p_2}\dots\binom{m-1}{p_s}$$
$$+ \binom{m}{2}\binom{m-2}{p_1}\binom{m-2}{p_2}\dots\binom{m-2}{p_s} - \dots .$$

To verify the special case $m = 3,\ p_1 = 3,\ p_2 = 2,\ p_3 = 1,$ we find

$$\binom{3}{3}\binom{3}{2}\binom{3}{1} = 9.$$

The more general condition that no object is to appear more than k times in the same box is treated by means of new functions

$$k_1, \ k_2, \ k_3, \ \ldots,$$

such that k_s is derived from h_s by striking out from the latter all partitions which contain parts greater than k. We then operate through the medium of compositions which contain no part greater than k and we reach a general solution analogous to those which employed the h and a functions.

CHAPTER IV

DISTRIBUTION WHEN OBJECTS AND BOXES ARE EQUAL IN NUMBER

40. We now come to an important case of distribution which is of particular interest in view of the light that it throws upon the algebra of symmetric functions. We consider a number of objects and an equal number of boxes. We are given the specifications both of the objects and of the boxes and place one object in each box. How many distributions are there?

Suppose that q_1 of the boxes are precisely similar, so that they have the specification (q_1). Whatever may be the specification of the q_1 objects that are placed in them it is certain that they have only one distribution, because the boxes being identical no permutation of the objects alters the distribution. Denote these boxes each by A_1. The specification of the q_1 objects must be one of the partitions which occur in h_{q_1} when expressed in terms of monomial functions. As one distribution we may take any product of $\alpha, \beta, \gamma, \dots$ that occurs in h_{q_1}. Also if there be q_2 boxes, each denoted by A_2, one distribution into the q_2 boxes will be any product of $\alpha, \beta, \gamma, \dots$ that occurs in h_{q_2}. And similarly for the boxes $q_3, q_4, \dots q_t$. Hence we write down the factors of the product

$$h_{q_1} h_{q_2} \dots h_{q_t},$$

each factor being written out in full, and obtain a distribution by taking any term of h_{q_1} for the q_1 boxes A_1, any term of h_{q_2} for the q_2 boxes A_2, etc. … any term of h_{q_t} for the q_t boxes A_t. If these terms when assembled constitute a combination which has the specification

$$(p_1 p_2 \dots p_s)$$

we will have one instance of a distribution of objects of specification $(p_1 p_2 \dots p_s)$ into boxes of specification $(q_1 q_2 \dots q_t)$, one object being in each box. It follows that the objects denoted by

$$a_1{}^{p_1} a_2{}^{p_2} \dots a_s{}^{p_s}$$

can be distributed into the boxes just as often as the term $a_1{}^{p_1} a_2{}^{p_2} \dots a_s{}^{p_s}$ arises in the product $h_{q_1} h_{q_2} \dots h_{q_t}$. The enumeration of the distributions is therefore given by the coefficient of the function $(p_1 p_2 \dots p_s)$ in the development of $h_{q_1} h_{q_2} \dots h_{q_t}$ in a series of monomial symmetric functions. We have the theorem :—

"The number of ways of distributing n objects of specification $(p_1 p_2 \ldots p_s)$ into n boxes of specification $(q_1 q_2 \ldots q_t)$, one object into each box, is equal to the coefficient of symmetric function $(p_1 p_2 \ldots p_s)$ in the development of the product $h_{q_1} h_{q_2} \ldots h_{q_t}$."

As an example, if $(p_1 p_2 \ldots p_s) = (411)$, $(q_1 q_2 \ldots q_t) = (321)$, one distribution is

$A_1\ A_1\ A_1$	$A_2\ A_2$	A_3
$a\quad a\quad a$	$a\quad \beta$	γ

corresponding to the terms a^3, $a\beta$, γ in h_3, h_2, h_1 respectively. The number of distributions is from previous work

$$D_4 D_1^2 h_3 h_2 h_1 = 8,$$

and the complete table of distributions is

$A_1\ A_1\ A_1$			$A_2\ A_2$		A_3
a	a	a	a	β	γ
a	a	a	a	γ	β
a	a	a	β	γ	a
a	a	β	a	a	γ
a	a	β	a	γ	a
a	a	γ	a	a	β
a	a	γ	a	β	a
a	β	γ	a	a	a

A table giving the development of products of the functions

$$h_1, \ h_2, \ h_3, \ \ldots$$

will give the complete numerical solution.

41. We now write the particular distribution we presented above in the form, writing A, B, C, ... for A_1, A_2, A_3, ...,

$A\ A\ A$	$B\ B$	C
$a\quad a\quad a$	$a\quad \beta$	γ

and observe that if we interchange the letters by writing A for a and a for A, B for β and β for B, C for γ and γ for C, we reach a distribution

$A\ A\ A\ A$	B	$C.$
$a\quad a\quad a\quad \beta$	β	γ

of objects of specification (321) into boxes of specification (411), and since we may transform every distribution in this way we obtain the theorem :—

"n objects of specification $(p_1 p_2 \ldots p_s)$ can be distributed into n boxes of specification $(q_1 q_2 \ldots q_t)$, one object in each box, in just as many ways as n objects of specification $(q_1 q_2 \ldots q_t)$ can be distributed into n boxes of specification $(p_1 p_2 \ldots p_s)$, one object in each box."

42. This quite obvious fact in the Theory of Distributions is next seen to lead to a Theorem of Symmetry in Algebra which is not only not obvious but was for a long time unsuspected.

If we denote by

$$C \begin{pmatrix} p_1 p_2 \cdots p_s \\ q_1 q_2 \cdots q_t \end{pmatrix}$$

the number of the distributions under examination we have shewn that

$$C \begin{pmatrix} p_1 p_2 \cdots p_s \\ q_1 q_2 \cdots q_t \end{pmatrix} = C \begin{pmatrix} q_1 q_2 \cdots q_t \\ p_1 p_2 \cdots p_s \end{pmatrix},$$

and this leads to the relation

$$D_{p_1} D_{p_2} \ldots D_{p_s} h_{q_1} h_{q_2} \ldots h_{q_t} = D_{q_1} D_{q_2} \ldots D_{q_t} h_{p_1} h_{p_2} \ldots h_{p_s},$$

or, in other words, the coefficient of symmetric function $(p_1 p_2 \ldots p_s)$ in the development of $h_{q_1} h_{q_2} \ldots h_{q_t}$ is equal to the coefficient of symmetric function $(q_1 q_2 \ldots q_t)$ in the development of $h_{p_1} h_{p_2} \ldots h_{p_s}$. This is called a 'Law of Symmetry,' because in a table which expresses the h products in terms of monomials for a given weight the rows will read the same as the columns. Thus such a table for the weight four is

	(4)	(31)	(2²)	(21²)	(1⁴)
h_4	1	1	1	1	1
$h_3 h_1$	1	2	2	3	4
$h_2{}^2$	1	2	3	4	6
$h_2 h_1{}^2$	1	3	4	7	12
$h_1{}^4$	1	4	6	12	24

43. If we look again at the distribution

$$\begin{array}{ccc} \underline{A\ A\ A} & \underline{B\ B} & C \\ a\ a\ a & a\ \beta & \gamma \end{array}$$

the symmetry that arises from the interchange of letters leads to the idea that instead of regarding the letters A, B, C as denoting boxes we may regard them as also denoting objects, but of a different kind from the objects denoted by a, β, γ; so that we may regard the distribution as being in fact a pairing of objects of two different sets of objects, one object being taken from each set to form a pair.

Observe that one set of objects involves no objects which appear in the other set. If the objects of both sets had been drawn from one set of objects, so that the objects in one set were not distinct from the objects in the other set, the distribution theory considered here would not be valid. For example, if we distribute the objects a, β, γ into the boxes A, B, C we obtain the six pairings of the objects a, β, γ with the objects A, B, C,

$$
\begin{array}{cccccc}
ABC & ABC & ABC & ABC & ABC & ABC \\
a\,\beta\,\gamma & a\,\gamma\,\beta & \beta\,a\,\gamma & \beta\,\gamma\,a & \gamma\,a\,\beta & \gamma\,\beta\,a
\end{array}
$$

but if we pair off the identical sets a, β, γ; a, β, γ, we obtain only the five pairings

$$
\begin{array}{ccccc}
a\beta\gamma & a\beta\gamma & a\beta\gamma & a\beta\gamma & a\beta\gamma \\
a\beta\gamma & a\gamma\beta & \beta a\gamma & \beta\gamma a & \gamma\beta a
\end{array}
$$

because the omitted pairing

$$
\begin{array}{c}
a\beta\gamma \\
\gamma a\beta
\end{array}
$$

is the same as

$$
\begin{array}{c}
a\beta\gamma \\
\beta\gamma a
\end{array}
$$

When any object in the one set also appears in the other we have a distribution, or pairing, which requires separate consideration, and indeed has been investigated up to a certain point*.

44. The distribution, regarded as a pairing off of sets of objects, which are distinct, is to be regarded as having a specification depending upon similarities of object-pairs. Thus the above pairing may be written

$$(Aa)^3 (Ba) (B\beta) (C\gamma),$$

which is said to have the specification (3111), which is also a partition of 6, the number of the objects distributed.

We may say that objects of specification (411) have been distributed into boxes of specification (321), one object in each box, in such wise that the specification of the distribution has the specification (3111).

* "Combinations derived from m identical sets of n different letters and their connexion with general magic squares," by Major ·P. A. MacMahon, *Proc. L. M. S.* Ser. 2, Vol. 17, Part ι.

Or, we may say that objects of specification (411) have been paired off with other objects of specification (321) in such wise that the specification of the object-pairs is (3111).

It is next to be noticed that the interchange of Capital and Greek letters does not alter the specification of the distribution. For looking at the object-pairing

$$(A\alpha)^3 (B\alpha)^1 (B\beta)^1 (C\gamma)^1,$$

it is clear that the interchange of letters cannot affect the repetitional numbers 3, 1, 1, 1, which are the parts of the partition which denote the specification.

45. We have before us clearly quite a new question, viz. the enumeration of distributions, of given specification, of objects of specification $(p_1 p_2 \ldots p_s)$ into boxes of specification $(q_1 q_2 \ldots q_t)$, one object into each box.

In Chapter v this question is considered up to a point. It has been solved completely in Combinatory Analysis. Suffice it to say that the theory has an important bearing upon the Algebra of Symmetric Functions. It establishes a refined law of symmetry connected with the partitions $(p_1 p_2 \ldots p_s)$, $(q_1 q_2 \ldots q_t)$, and the partition which denotes the distribution due to the circumstance that the first two of these partitions may be interchanged without altering the enumeration.

46. In the present theory the homogeneous product-sums $h_1, h_2, h_3, \ldots$ have appeared because no limit was imposed upon the number of times that similar objects may appear in similar boxes. Thus in boxes A, A, A, we have supposed it permissible to place objects represented by any of the terms $\alpha\alpha\alpha$, $\alpha\alpha\beta$, $\alpha\beta\gamma$, ... that compose h_3. The specifications of this portion of the distribution might be (3), (21) or (1^3). If we had resolved that not more than two similar objects were to be placed in similar boxes we could not have placed the objects α, α, α into the boxes A, A, A, and instead of the function h_3 we would have taken the function

$$(21) + (1^3),$$

and generally, in each of the functions $h_1, h_2, h_3, \ldots,$ we would have deleted all functions which in the partition notation are denoted by partitions which involve parts greater than 2. If the conditions be that not more than k similar objects are to be placed in similar boxes we substitute for $h_1, h_2, h_3, \ldots$ the corresponding set of functions $k_1, k_2, k_3, \ldots$ in which the deletion of partitions involving parts greater than k has been carried out. We then find that the number of distributions is equal to the coefficient of the function $(p_1 p_2 \ldots p_s)$ in the development of

$$k_{q_1} k_{q_2} \ldots k_{q_t},$$

and establish by interchange of Capital and Greek letters that the distributions, subject to the same condition, of objects of specification $(q_1 q_2 \ldots q_t)$ into boxes of specification $(p_1 p_2 \ldots p_s)$ are enumerated by the same number.

We thus see that the coefficient of $(p_1 p_2 \ldots p_s)$ in $k_{q_1} k_{q_2} \ldots k_{q_t}$ is equal to the coefficient of $(q_1 q_2 \ldots q_t)$ in $k_{p_1} k_{p_2} \ldots k^p{}_s$.

In other words we prove that

$$D_{p_1} D_{p_2} \ldots D_{p_s} k_{q_1} k_{q_2} \ldots k_{q_t} = D_{q_1} D_{q_2} \ldots D_{q_t} k_{p_1} k_{p_2} \ldots k_{p_s}.$$

Moreover, since

$$D_p h_m = h_{m-p},$$

also

$$D_p k_m = k_{m-p},$$

the evaluation of the coefficients can be carried out.

The specification of the distribution is clearly not altered by the interchange of Capital and Greek letters and we are led to an extended theory of symmetry in the Algebra of Symmetric Functions.

47. The case $k = 1$ is interesting because the homogeneous product-sums become the elementary functions

$$(1), (1^2), (1^3), \ldots \equiv a_1, a_2, a_3, \ldots,$$

and we establish that the coefficient of the function $(p_1 p_2 \ldots p_s)$ in the development of

$$a_{q_1} a_{q_2} \ldots a_{q_t}$$

is the same as that of $(q_1 q_2 \ldots q_t)$ in the development of

$$a_{p_1} a_{p_2} \ldots a_{p_s}.$$

This particular case of symmetric function symmetry has been known since the time of Meyer Hirsch early in the nineteenth century and several proofs have been given of it. That here given, based upon the theory of distribution, is the simplest and most suggestive. Since the specification of one of these distributions cannot involve any number greater than unity, we see that every distribution must have the same specification, viz. (1^n), where n is the number of objects. In the calculation the symbol D operates entirely through the medium of compositions of numbers which are composed entirely of units and zeros. This is so because

$$D_m (1^p) \equiv D_m a_p = \text{zero if } m \text{ be greater than unity.}$$

Thus

$$D_3 a_2 a_1{}^2 = D_3 (1^2)(1)(1) = D_1 (1^2) . D_1 (1) . D_1 (1) = (1),$$

$$D_2 (1^2)(1)(1) = D_1 (1^2) . D_1 (1) . D_0 (1) + D_1 (1^2) . D_0 (1) . D_1 (1)$$
$$+ D_0 (1^2) . D_1 (1) . D_1 (1)$$
$$= 2 (1)^2 + (1^2),$$

$$D_1 (1^2)(1)(1) = D_1 (1^2) . D_0 (1) . D_0 (1) + D_0 (1^2) . D_1 (1) . D_0 (1)$$
$$+ D_0 (1^2) . D_0 (1) . D_1 (1)$$
$$= (1)^3 + 2 (1^2)(1).$$

48. It has been established that the number

$$D_{p_1} D_{p_2} \dots D_{p_s} h_{q_1} h_{q_2} \dots h_{q_t}$$

enumerates distributions of objects into boxes when the distributions
are subject to certain conditions.

We can now shew, by reasoning upon the method of obtaining this
result, that the same number enumerates certain arithmetical construc-
tions of quite a different nature. When D_{p_1} operates upon $h_{q_1} h_{q_2} \dots h_{q_t}$
it acts through a number of compositions of p_1 into t parts, zero counting as a part. In this way we obtain the sum of a number of products
of which the type is

$$h_{q_1 - c_1} h_{q_2 - c_2} \dots h_{q_t - c_t},$$

where $c_1 c_2 \dots c_t$ is a composition of p_1.

Each of these products has unity for coefficient.

Restricting attention to the product above written the operation of
D_{p_2} is performed through compositions of p_2, and we obtain from the
one product we are attending to a number of products of which the
type is

$$h_{q_1 - c_1 - d_1} h_{q_2 - c_2 - d_2} \dots h_{q_t - c_t - d_t},$$

where $d_1 d_2 \dots d_t$ is a composition of p_2.

Each of these products has unity for coefficient.

Restricting the attention to this last written product the operation
of D_{p_3} yields a number of products of which

$$h_{q_1 - c_1 - d_1 - e_1} h_{q_2 - c_2 - d_2 - e_2} \dots h_{q_t - c_t - d_t - e_t}$$

is the type, where $e_1 e_2 \dots e_t$ is a composition of p_3.

Each of these products has unity for coefficient.

Finally, by this process, when we operate with D_{p_s} through one of
the compositions of p_s, viz.

$$\sigma_1 \sigma_2 \dots \sigma_t,$$

we reach the product

$$1 \times h_0 h_0 \dots h_0 \equiv 1.$$

We will then have arrived at the enumeration of one of our distributions through the medium of the succession of compositions

$$c_1 c_2 \ldots c_t, \quad d_1 d_2 \ldots d_t, \quad e_1 e_2 \ldots e_t, \quad \ldots\ldots \quad \sigma_1 \sigma_2 \ldots \sigma_t,$$

of the numbers p_1, p_2, p_3, $\ldots p_s$ respectively.

We may say that the particular distribution thus enumerated is in
correspondence with the numbered diagram

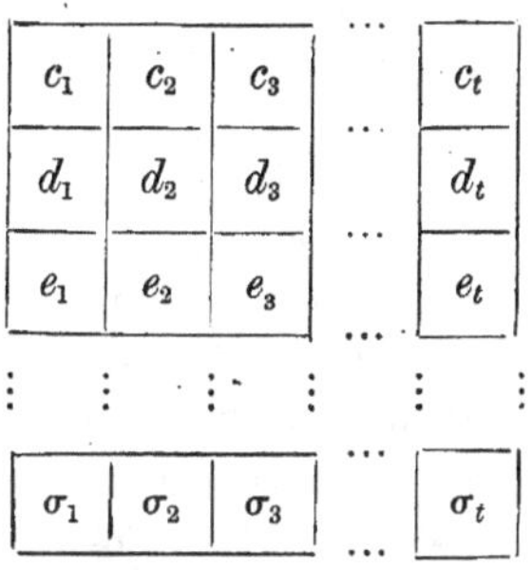

which involves a rectangle of s rows and t columns.

What is the definition of this diagram? Clearly the sums of the
numbers in the successive rows must be p_1, p_2, p_3, $\ldots p_s$ respectively,
and the sums of the numbers in the successive columns must be
q_1, q_2, q_3, $\ldots q_t$ respectively. The numbers must be positive integers
(zero included) and there is no restriction upon the magnitude.

To every such diagram also there corresponds one distribution.
Hence the number

$$D_{p_1} D_{p_2} \ldots D_{p_s} h_{q_1} h_{q_2} \ldots h_{q_t}$$

enumerates the diagrams so defined.

To take a very simple example, the number

$$D_2^2 h_2 h_1^2 = 4$$

enumerates the diagrams

2	0	0
0	1	1

1	1	0
1	0	1

1	0	1
1	1	0

0	1	1
2	0	0

where the rows add up to 2, 2 and the columns to 2, 1, 1.

49. We have an analogous enumeration also when the condition is
that not more than k similar objects are to be placed in similar boxes.

In every case the reciprocity that exists between the specifications
of the objects and of the boxes can be exhibited by rotating the diagrams through a right angle.

These identities of enumeration are simple instances of a very extensive theory in Combinatory Analysis.

50. Before closing this chapter it may be remarked that the placing of objects of any specification in boxes which are identical, one object in each box, is equivalent from a distribution point of view to placing the same objects in a single box. In both cases the objects can be permuted in any manner without changing the enumeration. There is in fact only one distribution. Consider then a distribution such that q_1 objects are placed in q_1 similar boxes A_1, q_2 objects in q_2 similar boxes A_2, ... q_t objects in similar boxes A_t, the sets of objects having any specifications and one object being in each box. In contrast with this consider the q_1, q_2, ... q_t objects placed in *single* boxes B_1, B_2, ... B_t respectively. If the numbers q_1, q_2, ... q_t be all different we cannot in the first distribution interchange any pair of the sets of q_1, q_2, ... q_t objects because, for example, the q_r objects will only fit into the q_r similar boxes A_r. Also in the second distribution if the boxes B_1, B_2, ... B_t be identical we cannot alter the distribution by any interchange of a pair of the sets of q_1, q_2, ... q_t objects. Hence there is a one-to-one correspondence and we may state that the number of distributions of objects of specification $(p_1 p_2 \ldots p_s)$ into boxes of specification $(q_1 q_2 \ldots q_t)$, *the numbers q_1, q_2, ... q_t being all different*, one object being placed in each box, is equal to the number of distributions of objects of specification $(p_1 p_2 \ldots p_s)$ into boxes of specification (t) such that the t boxes contain q_1, q_2, ... q_t objects respectively. For example, compare these distributions where

$$(p_1 p_2 \ldots p_s) = (321), \quad (q_1 q_2 \ldots q_t) = (321),$$

$$\underline{A_1 A_1 A_1} \ \ \underline{A_2 A_2} \ \ \underline{A_3}$$

or

$\underline{A}$	$\underline{A}$	$\underline{A}$
$\alpha\beta\gamma$	$\alpha\beta$	α
$\alpha\beta\beta$	$\alpha\gamma$	α
$\alpha\alpha\gamma$	$\beta\beta$	α
$\beta\beta\gamma$	$\alpha\alpha$	α
$\alpha\alpha\beta$	$\beta\gamma$	α
$\alpha\beta\gamma$	$\alpha\alpha$	β
$\alpha\alpha\gamma$	$\alpha\beta$	β
$\alpha\alpha\beta$	$\alpha\gamma$	β
$\alpha\alpha\alpha$	$\beta\gamma$	β
$\alpha\alpha\alpha$	$\beta\beta$	γ
$\alpha\alpha\beta$	$\alpha\beta$	γ
$\alpha\beta\beta$	$\alpha\alpha$	γ

51. Again, if the numbers q_1, q_2, ... q_t be identical and the boxes B_1, B_2, ... B_t have the specification (1^t) we find that in the first distribution the sets of q_1, q_2, ... q_t objects can be permuted in all possible ways so as to produce new distributions—the number of ways depending upon the similarities that may exist between the t sets of objects. Also in the second distribution, since the boxes are all different, the sets of objects can be permuted exactly as in the first distribution, and we may say that the number of distributions of objects of specification $(p_1 p_2 \ldots p_s)$ into boxes of specification $(q_1 q_2 \ldots q_t)$, *the numbers q_1, q_2, ... q_t being identical*, one object being placed in each box, is equal to the number of distributions of objects of specification $(p_1 p_2 \ldots p_s)$ into boxes of specification (1^t) such that the t boxes contain in some order q_1, q_2, ... q_t objects respectively. As an example we may compare the distributions of objects of specification (321) into the boxes

$$A_1 A_1 \ A_2 A_2 \ A_3 A_3 \ \text{and} \ A_1 A_2 A_3,$$

where $(p_1 p_2 \ldots p_s) = (321)$, $(q_1 q_2 \ldots q_t) = (222)$.

CHAPTER V

DISTRIBUTIONS OF GIVEN SPECIFICATION

52. In this chapter we examine the distribution theory that has just been before us with special reference to the specifications of the distributions. In a product-sum such as h_3, for example

$$(3) + (21) + (1^3),$$

the occurrence of a part 1, 2, or 3 in a partition indicates that 1, 2, or 3 similar parts have been placed in similar boxes and it was by restricting the magnitude of these parts to be not greater than k that we were able to determine the theory of the distribution when the condition was that not more than k similar objects were to be placed in similar boxes. In order to put in evidence the specifications of the distributions we consider in connexion with the product-sums $h_1, h_2, h_3, \ldots$ the new functions

$$X_1 = x_1(1),$$
$$X_2 = x_2(2) + x_1^2(1^2),$$
$$X_3 = x_3(3) + x_2 x_1(21) + x_1^3(1^3),$$
$$X_4 = x_4(4) + x_3 x_1(31) + x_2^2(2^2) + x_2 x_1^2(21^2) + x_1^4(1^4).$$

We may if we choose regard $x_1, x_2, x_3, \ldots$ as being the elementary symmetric functions of a new set of elements

$$a', \beta', \gamma', \ldots.$$

Indicating symmetric functions of this set by dashed brackets, viz. $(\quad)'$, the relations may be written

$$X_1 = (1)'(1),$$
$$X_2 = (1^2)'(2) + (2)'(1^2) + 2(1^2)'(1^2),$$
$$X_3 = (1^3)'(3) + 2(1^3)'(21) + (21)'(21) + 6(1^3)'(1^3)$$
$$+ (3)'(1^3) + 2(21)'(1^3),$$
$$\text{etc.}$$

and we, at once, notice a symmetry in the right-hand sides of these relations. They are unaltered by an interchange of dashed and undashed brackets or in other words, by an interchange of the sets of quantities $a, \beta, \gamma, \ldots a', \beta', \gamma', \ldots$. To prove that this symmetry is universal consider the infinite series

$$1 + X_1 + X_2 + X_3 + \ldots,$$

which is expressible as the product

$$(1 + x_1 a + x_2 a^2 + x_3 a^3 + \ldots)$$
$$\times (1 + x_1 \beta + x_2 \beta^2 + x_3 \beta^3 + \ldots)$$
$$\times (1 + x_1 \gamma + x_2 \gamma^2 + x_3 \gamma^3 + \ldots)$$
$$\times \ldots,$$

because the coefficient of $x_\lambda x_\mu x_\nu \ldots$ therein is

$$\Sigma\, a^\lambda \beta^\mu \gamma^\nu \ldots \equiv (\lambda\mu\nu\ldots).$$

Since x_1, x_2, x_3, ... are the elementary functions of a', β', γ', ...

$$(1 + x_1 a + x_2 a^2 + x_3 a^3 + \ldots) = (1 + a'a)(1 + \beta'a)(1 + \gamma'a)\ldots,$$

so that also

$$1 + X_1 + X_2 + X_3 + \ldots$$
$$= (1 + a'a)(1 + \beta'a)(1 + \gamma'a)\ldots$$
$$\times (1 + a'\beta)(1 + \beta'\beta)(1 + \gamma'\beta)\ldots$$
$$\times (1 + a'\gamma)(1 + \beta'\gamma)(1 + \gamma'\gamma)\ldots$$
$$\times \ldots;$$

a relation which establishes the symmetry for the right-hand side is unaltered by the interchange of dashed and undashed letters.

53. We have to deal at present with the set of relations which commences with $X_1 = x_1(1)$.

Taking any product of the functions X, say for example $X_4 X_3$, we find that we can arrange the right-hand side according to products of quantities x_1, x_2, x_3,.... In particular, selecting the term which involves $x_3 x_2 x_1^2$, we have

$$X_4 X_3 = \ldots + \{(21^2)(3) + (31)(21)\}\, x_3 x_2 x_1^2 + \ldots.$$

The function

$$(21^2)(3) + (31)(21)$$

is associated with two partitions of the number 7; (43) which defines the X product and (321^2) which defines the x product. The numbers which appear in the two functions $(21^2)(3)$, $(31)(21)$ are those which appear in the x product and moreover each function involves partitions of the numbers 4, 3 which appear in the X product.

The symmetric function products $(21^2)(3)$, $(31)(21)$ are derived from the symmetric function (321^2) by a process called 'Separation' and each is said to be a 'Separation' of (321^2). Each factor of such a product is said to be a 'Separate' of the 'Separation.' The like terms are employed when we are thinking only of Partitions. A partition is separated into separates just as a number is partitioned into parts.

Separation consists in separating combinations of parts by distinct brackets. Thus

$$(321^2), (321)(1), (31^2)(2), (32)(1^2), (21^2)(3), (31)(21), (32)(1)^2,$$
$$(31)(2)(1), (3)(21)(1), (3)(2)(1^2),$$
$$(3)(2)(1)^2, \quad \ldots$$

are all separations alike of the function (321^2) and of the partition (321^2).

We may therefore say that the two terms of $(21^2)(3) + (31)(21)$ are, both, separations of the function (321^2).

A separation has a specification which consists of the series of numbers which denote the sums of the numbers in separate brackets or as we may say in the separates. Thus the eleven separations above written have specifications

$$(7), (61), (52), (52), (43), (43), (51^2),$$
$$(421), (3^21), (32^2),$$
$$(321^2).$$

Hence the terms of $(21^2)(3) + (31)(21)$ may be fully described as being separations, of the partition (321^2) which defines the x product, which have the specification (43) which defines the X product. The terms $(21^2)(3), (31)(21)$ each appear above with the coefficient unity because in the associated X product no exponent exceeds unity. Had we chosen the product $X_3^2 X_2^3$ we would have obtained a term

$$2(3)(21) \cdot 3(2)^2(1^2) \ x_3 x_2^3 x_1^3$$

such that $(3)(21)(2)^2(1^2)$ is a separation of (32^31^3) of specification (3^22^3) and the coefficient 3×2 that presents itself denotes that the separation $(2)^2(1^2)$, composed of separates of the same weight, has three permutations; and similarly that the separation $(3)(21)$, also composed of separates of the same weight, has two permutations.

We may say that in the X product the coefficient of a separation is equal to the number of permutations of the separates when only permutations between separates of the same weight are permitted.

54. Take now the general X product

$$X_{q_1} X_{q_2} \ldots X_{q_t} = + P \, x_{\sigma_1} x_{\sigma_2} x_{\sigma_3} \ldots + \ldots.$$

We see that

(i) P is a linear function of separations of $(\sigma_1 \sigma_2 \sigma_3 \ldots)$.

(ii) Each separation that appears has the specification $(q_1 q_2 \ldots q_t)$ and every such separation presents itself.

(iii) The numerical coefficient of a separation is equal to the number of permutations of its separates when only permutations between separates of the same weight are permitted.

We now expand P in a series of monomials so that

$$P = \ldots + \theta\,(p_1 p_2 \ldots p_s) + \ldots$$

and

$$X_{q_1} X_{q_2} \ldots X_{q_t} = \ldots + \theta\,(p_1 p_2 \ldots p_s)\, x_{\sigma_1} x_{\sigma_2} x_{\sigma_3} \ldots.$$

We gather that objects of specification

$$(p_1 p_2 \ldots p_s)$$

can be distributed into boxes of specification

$$(q_1 q_2 \ldots q_t),$$

one object in each box, so that the distributions have, all, the specification

$$(\sigma_1 \sigma_2 \sigma_3 \ldots)$$

in θ ways.

55. It has been seen in the foregoing chapter that we can interchange the specifications of the objects and boxes without altering the specifications of the distributions or the number θ. Hence we have a law of algebraic symmetry indicated by the complementary formula

$$X_{p_1} X_{p_2} \ldots X_{p_s} = \ldots + \theta\,(q_1 q_2 \ldots q_t)\, x_{\sigma_1} x_{\sigma_2} x_{\sigma_3} \ldots + \ldots.$$

As an example we develop the term

$$\{(21^2)(3) + (31)(21)\}\, x_3 x_2 x_1^2,$$

which appears in the product $X_4 X_3$, and we find

$$X_4 X_3 = \ldots + \{(52) + 3\,(51^2) + (43) + 2\,(421) + 2\,(3^2 1)$$
$$+ 2\,(32^2) + 3\,(321^2)\}\, x_3 x_2 x_1^2 + \ldots$$

and we interpret any particular term, say $3\,(51^2)$, by stating that objects of specification (51^2) can be distributed into boxes of specification (43), one object in each box, in such wise that the distribution has a specification (321^2) in 3 ways. These are in fact

A	A	A	A	B	B	B
a	a	a	β	a	a	γ
a	a	a	γ	a	a	β
a	a	β	γ	a	a	a

the specifications of the distributions being shewn by

$$\frac{A\ \ A\ \ A}{a\ \ a\ \ a}\bigg|\frac{B\ \ B}{a\ \ a}\bigg|\frac{A}{\beta}\bigg|\frac{B}{\gamma} \qquad \frac{A\ \ A\ \ A}{a\ \ a\ \ a}\bigg|\frac{B\ \ B}{a\ \ a}\bigg|\frac{A}{\gamma}\bigg|\frac{B}{\beta}$$

$$\frac{B\ \ B\ \ B}{a\ \ a\ \ a}\bigg|\frac{A\ \ A}{a\ \ a}\bigg|\frac{A}{\beta}\bigg|\frac{A}{\gamma}$$

56. To shew the reciprocity we calculate

$$X_5 X_1^{\,2} = \ldots + 3\,(43)\,x_3 x_2 x_1^{\,2} + \ldots,$$

and the distributions are

A	A	A	A	A	B	C
a	a	a	β	β	a	β
a	a	a	β	β	β	a
a	a	β	β	β	a	a

3 in number and each of specification (321^2).

57. The symbol D_m can be employed with good effect because if we operate upon

$$X_{q_1} X_{q_2} \ldots X_{qt}$$

with

$$D_{p_1} D_{p_2} \ldots D_{p_s},$$

we obtain a linear function of x products which gives a complete specification account of the distributions of the objects into the boxes.

We proceed from the relation

$$D_s X_q = x_s X_{q-s},$$

valid for all integer values of s and also when $s = 0$ if we put $x_0 = 1$.

To take an example consider objects and boxes of the specifications $(2^2 1^3)$, (43) respectively and recall the way in which the symbol D_m operates upon a product through the compositions of its suffix. The calculation is

$$D_2^{\,2} D_1^{\,3} X_4 X_3$$
$$= D_2 D_1^{\,3}\,(x_2 X_3 X_2 + x_2 X_4 X_1 + x_1^{\,2} X_3 X_2)$$
$$= D_1^{\,3}\{(x_2 + x_1^{\,2})\,(x_2 X_3 + x_2 X_2 X_1 + x_1^{\,2} X_2 X_1)$$
$$\qquad\qquad\qquad\qquad + x_2\,(x_2 X_2 X_1 + x_1^{\,2} X_3)\}$$
$$= D_1^{\,3}\{(x_2^{\,2} + 2x_2 x_1^{\,2})\,X_3 + (2x_2^{\,2} + 2x_2 x_1^{\,2} + x_1^{\,4})\,X_2 X_1\}$$
$$= D_1^{\,2}\{(x_2^{\,2} x_1 + 2x_2 x_1^{\,3})\,X_2 + (2x_2^{\,2} x_1 + 2x_2 x_1^{\,3} + x_1^{\,5})\,X_2$$
$$\qquad\qquad\qquad\qquad + (2x_2^{\,2} x_1 + 2x_2 x_1^{\,3} + x_1^{\,5})\,X_1^{\,2}\}$$
$$= D_1^{\,2}\{(3x_2^{\,2} x_1 + 4x_2 x_1^{\,3} + x_1^{\,5})\,X_2 + (2x_2^{\,2} x_1 + 2x_2 x_1^{\,3} + x_1^{\,5})\,X_1^{\,2}\}$$
$$= D_1\,(7x_2^{\,2} x_1^{\,2} + 8x_2 x_1^{\,4} + 3x_1^{\,6})\,X_1$$
$$= 7x_2^{\,2} x_1^{\,3} + 8x_2 x_1^{\,5} + 3x_1^{\,7},$$

and the distributions indicated are

Spec. $(2^2 1^3)$

A	A	A	A	B	B	B
a	a	β	β	γ	δ	ϵ
a	a	γ	δ	β	β	ϵ
a	a	γ	ϵ	β	β	δ
a	a	δ	ϵ	β	β	γ
γ	δ	β	β	a	a	ϵ
γ	ϵ	β	β	a	a	δ
δ	ϵ	β	β	a	a	γ

No. 7

Spec. (21^5)

A	A	A	A	B	B	B
a	$\dot{a}$	β	γ	β	δ	ϵ
a	a	β	δ	β	γ	ϵ
a	a	β	ϵ	β	γ	δ
a	γ	β	β	a	δ	ϵ
a	δ	β	β	a	γ	ϵ
a	ϵ	β	β	a	γ	δ
a	γ	δ	ϵ	a	β	β
β	γ	δ	ϵ	a	a	β

No. 8

Spec. (1^7)

A	A	A	A	B	B	B
a	β	γ	δ	a	β	ϵ
a	β	γ	ϵ	a	β	δ
a	β	δ	ϵ	a	β	γ

No. 3

58. It will be observed that, since $D_s X_q = x_s X_{q-s}$, the x product of highest degree obtained from

$$D_{p_1} D_{p_2} \ldots D_{p_s} X_{q_1} X_{q_2} \ldots X_{q_t}$$

must be

$$x_{p_1} x_{p_2} \ldots x_{p_s}.$$

Again from the symmetry on the right-hand sides of the relations

$$X_1 = x_1(1),$$
$$X_2 = x_2(2) + x_1^{2}(1^2),$$
$$X_3 = x_3(3) + x_2 x_1(21) + x_1^{3}(1^3),$$

which was established in Art. 52, we may derive from the relation

$$D_s X_q = x_s X_{q-s}$$

the relation

$$D_s' X_q = a_s X_{q-s}$$

where the symbol D_s' has reference to the symmetric functions of the quantities $a', \beta', \gamma', \ldots$ and as before $a_1, a_2, a_3, \ldots$ are the elementary functions of the quantities $a, \beta, \gamma, \ldots$.

This is so because an interchange of the sets

$$a, \beta, \gamma, \ldots, \qquad a', \beta', \gamma', \ldots$$

leaves X_q and X_{q-s} unaltered while changing D_s into D_s' and x_s into a_s.

Similarly from the result

$$D_2^2 D_1^3 X_4 X_3 = 7x_1^3 x_2^2 + 8x_1^5 x_2 + 3x_1^7,$$

we derive

$$D_2'^2 D_1'^3 X_4 X_3 = 7a_1^3 a_2^2 + 8a_1^5 a_2 + 3a_1^7.$$

These transformations are of much service in the development of the algebra.

59. In Art. 55 we have determined the specifications of the distributions when we are given the specifications of the objects and boxes. We can obtain all the distributions which have a given specification, the specifications of the objects and boxes being at disposal by simply expanding an X product as a linear function of x products. Thus since

$$X_2^2 = x_2^2 \{(4) + 2\,(2^2)\} + x_2 x_1^2 \{2\,(31) + 2\,(21^2)\}$$
$$+ x_1^4 \{(2^2) + 2\,(21^2) + 6\,(1^4)\}$$

we gather that a distribution of specification (2^2) can be obtained, when the box specification is (2^2), by distributing objects of specification (4) in one way, and objects of specification (2^2) in two ways; and similarly the other two terms upon the right-hand side can be interpreted.

The distributions are

(2^2)

	A	A	B	B
(4)	a	a	a	a
(2^2)	a	a	β	β
	β	β	a	a

(21^2)

	A	A	B	B
(31)	a	a	a	β
	a	β	a	a
(21^2)	a	a	β	γ
	β	γ	a	a

(1^4)

	A	A	B	B
(2^2)	a	β	a	β
(21^2)	a	β	a	γ
	a	γ	a	β
	a	β	γ	δ
	a	γ	β	δ
(1^4)	a	δ	β	γ
	β	γ	a	δ
	β	δ	a	γ
	γ	δ	a	β

60. In Art. 48 we shewed that the theory of a certain distribution led easily to the enumeration of certain numbered diagrams which could be accurately defined. The correspondence was obtained by an examination of the way in which the operation of the symbol D_m is effective in obtaining the enumerating number. Looking back to Art. 57 we can similarly examine the calculation involved in the expression

$$D_2^2 D_1^3 X_4 X_3.$$

The symbol D_m is performed through the medium of the compositions of the number m. If

$$c_1,\ c_2,\ \dots c_t$$

be such a composition we may have to perform the symbols

$$D_{c_1},\ D_{c_2},\ D_{c_3},\ \dots D_{c_t}$$

upon the several factors of the X product. Now since (Art. 57)

$$D_s X_q = x_s X_{q-s}$$

we see that, associated with the particular portion of the operation, we will have a product

$$x_{c_1}\, x_{c_2} \cdots x_{c_t}$$

with coefficient unity, and not merely unity as is the case when we are dealing with the functions $h_1, h_2, h_3, \ldots$.

Again operating as in Art. 48 through another composition $d_1, d_2, \ldots d_t$ we obtain another x factor

$$x_{d_1}\, x_{d_2} \cdots x_{d_t}$$

the coefficient being again unity.

Finally we arrive at a certain x product with the coefficient unity and we find that corresponding to one of the distributions we have a lettered diagram

x_{c_1}	x_{c_2}	x_{c_3}	$\cdots$	x_{c_t}
x_{d_1}	x_{d_2}	x_{d_3}		x_{d_t}
x_{e_1}	x_{e_2}	x_{e_3}		x_e
$\vdots$	$\vdots$	$\vdots$	$\vdots$	$\vdots$
x_{s_1}	x_{s_2}	x_{s_3}	$\cdots$	$x_{s}{}^t$

and the product of these st, x factors defines the specification of the particular distribution which has led us to this diagram. Eliminating the symbol x from the diagram, as it has no numerical significance, we write it

c_1	c_2	c_3	$\cdots$	c_t
d_1	d_2	d_3		d_t
e_1	e_2	e_3		e_t
$\vdots$	$\vdots$	$\vdots$	$\vdots$	$\vdots$
s_1	s_2	s_3	$\cdots$	s_t

If the distributions considered have, all of them, the same specification defined by the x product resulting from the diagram, it is clear that the diagrams must all give the product $x_{\sigma_1} x_{\sigma_2} x_{\sigma_3} \ldots$, where the partition $(\sigma_1\sigma_2\sigma_3 \ldots)$ is the specification of the distributions. Hence the numbers $c_1,\ c_2,\ \ldots d_1,\ d_2,\ \ldots s_1,\ s_2,\ \ldots$ in the numbered diagrams must, when assembled, make up the partition $(\sigma_1\sigma_2\sigma_3 \ldots)$.

We may therefore state the theorem :—

"Let there be a rectangular chess-board of t columns and s rows and let given numbers $\sigma_1,\ \sigma_2,\ \ldots \sigma_\tau,\ \tau$ in number, be placed in the compartments in such wise that the sums of the numbers in the successive rows are $p_1,\ p_2,\ \ldots p_s$ and in the successive columns $q_1,\ q_2,\ \ldots q_t$; then the number of such numbered chess-boards is equal to the number of ways of distributing objects of specification $(p_1 p_2 \ldots p_s)$ into boxes of specification $(q_1 q_2 \ldots q_t)$ subject to the condition that the distributions are to have the specification $(\sigma_1\sigma_2 \ldots \sigma_t)$."

61. As an example, by means of the result

$$D_2^2 D_1^3 X_4 X_3 = 7x_1^3 x_2^2 + 8x_1^5 x_2 + 3x_1^7,$$

we enumerate the 7 diagrams

Diagram 1:

2	
2	
	1
	1
	1

Diagram 2:

2	
	2
1	
1	
	1

Diagram 3:

2	
	2
1	
	1
1	

Diagram 4:

2	
	2
	1
1	
1	

Diagram 5:

	2
2	
1	
1	
	1

Diagram 6:

	2
2	
1	
	1
1	

Diagram 7:

	2
2	
	1
1	
1	

in which the compartment numbers are 2, 2, 1, 1, 1 derived from the specification $(2^2 1^3)$ of the corresponding distributions; the row sums are 2, 2, 1, 1, 1 derived from the specification $(2^2 1^3)$ of the objects distributed, and the column sums are 4, 3 derived from the specification (43) of the boxes.

Also we enumerate the 8 diagrams

Diagram 1:

2	
1	1
1	
	1
	1

Diagram 2:

2	
1	1
	1
1	
	1

Diagram 3:

2	
1	1
	1
	1
1	

Diagram 4:

1	1
2	
1	
	1
	1

Diagram 5:

1	1
2	
	1
1	
	1

Diagram 6:

1	1
2	
	1
	1
1	

Diagram 7:

1	1
	2
1	
1	
1	

Diagram 8:

	2
1	1
1	
1	
1	

associated with the compartment numbers 2, 1, 1, 1, 1, 1, and the 3 diagrams

associated with the compartment numbers 1, 1, 1, 1, 1, 1, 1, the row and column sums being, as before, derived from the partitions $(2^2 1^3)$, (43). (Compare Art. 49.)

CHAPTER VI

THE MOST GENERAL·CASE OF DISTRIBUTION

62. So far two main divisions of the Theory of Distribution have been under consideration, viz. the case in which there are no similarities between the boxes and the case in which the number of boxes is equal to the number of objects. In the former the objects may be of any specification; in the latter both the objects and the boxes may be of any specification. The next main division that presents itself for examination is concerned with boxes which may be any in number but in every case indistinguishable from one another. They have the specification (m) when they are m in number. The objects may be any in number and of any specification. No box is supposed to be left empty so that the objects are at least as numerous as the boxes.

Objects of the specification $(p_1 p_2 \ldots p_s)$ are in correspondence with the assemblage of letters

$$a_1{}^{p_1} a_2{}^{p_2} \ldots a_s{}^{p_s} \text{ or } a^{p_1} \beta^{p_2} \ldots \sigma^{p_s} \text{ or } a^p \beta^q \gamma^r \ldots .$$

63. The partition $(p_1 p_2 \ldots p_s)$ may, from another standpoint, be regarded as a multipartite number or, in other words, as a succession of numbers which enumerate letters or objects of different kinds.

If we separate any combination of letters from the assemblage

$$a^p \beta^q \gamma^r \ldots ,$$

say
$$a^{p_1} \beta^{q_1} \gamma^{r_1} \ldots ,$$

the numbers $p_1,\ q_1,\ r_1,\ \ldots$ are not necessarily or generally in descending order of magnitude and some of them may be zeros. If we break up the assemblage into m portions

$$a^{p_1} \beta^{q_1} \gamma^{r_1} \ldots , \quad a^{p_2} \beta^{q_2} \gamma^{r_2} \ldots , \quad \ldots a^{p_m} \beta^{q_m} \gamma^{r_m} \ldots ,$$

without any regard to the order of writing the portions, we may speak of a distribution of objects of specification $(pqr\ldots)$ into boxes of specification (m) because no permutation of the boxes, which are all similar, alters the distribution. In correspondence we speak of partitioning the multipartite number into m multipartite parts and we denote such partition by the notation

$$(p_1 q_1 r_1 \ldots , \quad p_2 q_2 r_2 \ldots , \quad \ldots p_m q_m r_m \ldots).$$

The parts may be placed in any order without affecting the partition.

Thence it arises that the problem of distribution into similar boxes is identical with that of partitioning a multipartite number.

It will be remarked that a collection of integers in a bracket may denote either a partition of an ordinary or unipartite number or a multipartite number, but that whereas the parts of the partition in the former case may always be written in descending order, such is not the case with the constituents of the multipartite parts of a multipartite number.

As a simple example of the correspondence between distribution and partition, take the assemblage $\alpha^2\beta^2$.

Distribution of $\alpha^2\beta^2$ into two similar boxes		Partitions of (22) into two parts
A	A	
$\alpha^2\beta$	β	(21, 01)
$\alpha\beta^2$	α	(12, 10)
α^2	β^2	(20, 02)
$\alpha\beta$	$\alpha\beta$	(11, 11)

64. In the main divisions previously discussed we have had to deal with the homogeneous product-sums of the elements α, β, γ, ... In the present main division we have also to deal with homogeneous product-sums, not of the simple elements but of certain combinations of them, u_1, u_2, u_3, ...

A reference to Art. 8 shews that we can arrive at the product-sums by first obtaining the power-sums.

Thus if
$$u_1{}^k + u_2{}^k + u_3{}^k + \ldots = \sigma_k,$$

and U_1, U_2, U_3, ... denote the product-sums,

$$U_1 = \sigma_1,$$
$$2! \, U_2 = \sigma_1{}^2 + \sigma_2,$$
$$3! \, U_3 = \sigma_1{}^3 + 3\sigma_1\sigma_2 + 2\sigma_3,$$
$$4! \, U_4 = \sigma_1{}^4 + 6\sigma_1{}^2\sigma_2 + 3\sigma_2{}^2 + 8\sigma_1\sigma_3 + 6\sigma_4,$$
$$\ldots\ldots\ldots\ldots\ldots\ldots\ldots\ldots\ldots\ldots\ldots\ldots$$
$$m! \, U_m = \Sigma \frac{m!}{m_1! \, m_2! \, m_3! \ldots} \left(\frac{\sigma_1}{1}\right)^{m_1} \left(\frac{\sigma_2}{2}\right)^{m_2} \left(\frac{\sigma_3}{3}\right)^{m_3} \ldots$$

We have to determine the particular combinations of α, β, γ, $\cdots$ that we may substitute for u_1, u_2, u_3, ..., so as to be of service in the problem before us.

If we take $m = 1$, so that there is but a single box, we note that for any assemblage of objects

$$\alpha^p \beta^q \gamma^r \dots$$

there is only one distribution; the whole of the objects must be placed in the only box. Hence the symmetric-function enumerating function must be the sum of all the monomial functions of all weights. We may take it to be

$$h_1 + h_2 + h_3 + \dots \text{ ad inf.}$$
$$\equiv (1) + (2) + (1^2) + (3) + (21) + (1^3) + \dots,$$

because the coefficient of the function $(pqr \dots)$ in the series of functions is unity.

When $m = 2$, we may place in the two boxes any two assemblages which, added together, make the assemblage to be distributed. Regarding

$$\alpha^p \beta^q \gamma^r \dots$$

as a literal product, we have two products whose product is equal to the given product. Now it is evident that if P_1, P_2 be two such products, the distribution must be of one of the *types*

$$\frac{A\ A}{P_1 P_1} \quad \frac{A\ A}{P_1 P_2}$$

so that the product distributed must be either P_1^2 or $P_1 P_2$, where P_1, P_2 separately may be any combination of letters. Hence every possible distribution will be realised for all specifications of the objects to be distributed by taking the product-sums of *order two* of all combinations of letters. The enumerating function must therefore be the sum of such product-sums of all weights.

Similarly when $m = 3$, the distribution must be of one of the types

$$\frac{A\ A\ A}{P_1 P_1 P_1} \quad \frac{A\ A\ A}{P_1 P_1 P_2} \quad \frac{A\ A\ A}{P_1 P_2 P_3}$$

so that the product to be distributed must be either P_1^3 or $P_1^2 P_2$ or $P_1 P_2 P_3$. Hence the enumerating function must be the sum of product-sums of *order three* of all combinations of letters.

By similar reasoning for m boxes the enumerating function must be the sum of product-sums of *order m* of all combinations of letters. These combinations are the terms of the infinite series

$$h_1 + h_2 + h_3 + \dots \text{ ad. inf.}$$

65. If we proceed now from these combinations we will obtain a solution of the problem, but it is much better to include unity in the series of terms. If unity may be placed in any box instead of one of the above combinations it is clear that we will enumerate the distributions into *m or fewer* boxes, and this will be quite satisfactory because we have only to subtract the function which enumerates the distributions into $m-1$ or fewer boxes in order to obtain the function which enumerates the distributions into m boxes, no box being empty. As the algebra is easier we adopt this course and put

$$S_1 = 1 + h_1 + h_2 + h_3 + \dots$$
$$\equiv 1 + (1) + (2) + (1^2) + (3) + (21) + (1^3) + \dots.$$

The sum of the kth powers S_k, of all the terms appearing herein, is obtained, as is readily realised, by multiplying every part which appears in the partitions by k.

Hence
$$S_2 = 1 + (2) + (4) + (2^2) + (6) + (42) + (2^3) + \dots,$$
$$S_3 = 1 + (3) + (6) + (3^2) + (9) + (63) + (3^3) + \dots,$$
$$\dots\dots\dots\dots\dots\dots\dots\dots\dots\dots\dots\dots\dots\dots\dots\dots\dots$$
$$S_k = 1 + (k) + (2k) + (k^2) + (3k) + (2k, k) + (k^3) + \dots,$$

and thence if U_1, U_2, U_3, ... be the product-sums,
$$U_1 = S_1,$$
$$2! \, U_2 = S_1^2 + S_2,$$
$$3! \, U_3 = S_1^3 + 3S_1 S_2 + 2S_3,$$
$$4! \, U_4 = S_1^4 + 6S_1^2 S_2 + 3S_2^2 + 8S_1 S_3 + 6S_4,$$
$$\dots\dots\dots\dots\dots\dots\dots\dots\dots\dots\dots\dots\dots\dots\dots\dots$$
$$m! \, U_m = \Sigma \frac{m!}{m_1! \, m_2! \, m_3! \dots} \left(\frac{S_1}{1}\right)^{m_1} \left(\frac{S_2}{2}\right)^{m_2} \left(\frac{S_3}{3}\right)^{m_3} \dots.$$

This is the expression of the enumerating function U_m in which the coefficient of the function $(pqr\dots)$ is to be taken.

66. If, on development, we find that
$$U_m = \dots + \theta \, (pqr\dots) + \dots,$$
our operating symbols shew us that
$$D_p D_q D_r \dots U_m = \theta D_p D_q D_r \dots (pqr\dots) = \theta,$$
since no other terms on the right-hand side survive the operations. We must therefore learn how to operate with the D symbol. It will be remembered that the symbol D_m causes every symmetric function, whose partition does not involve the number m, to vanish, and that

when the number m does appéar it strikes out that number from the partition once. Now the portion of S_1, that involves m in partitions, is

$$(m) + (m1) + (m2) + (m1^2) + (m3) + (m21) + (m1^3) + \dots \text{ ad. inf.}$$

Hence $\qquad\qquad\qquad\qquad D_m S_1 = S_1,$

or every operative symbol leaves S_1 unaltered.

Also $\qquad\qquad\qquad D_{2m} S_2 = S_2, \quad D_{2m+1} S_2 = 0,$

since S_2 does not involve any uneven number.

Generally $D_{im} S_i = S_i$ and $D_s S_i = 0$ unless s is a multiple of i.

The effect of D_m upon $S_1^{k_1}$ comes next for consideration. The symbol operates through the compositions of m into k_1 parts, zero being included as a possible part.

Thus for example, omitting the operator D_0 for convenience, replacing $D_0 S_1$ by its value S_1,

$$\begin{aligned}
D_3 S_1^3 &= D_3 S_1 . S_1 . S_1 + S_1 . D_3 S_1 . S_1 + S_1 . S_1 . D_3 S_1 \\
&\quad + D_2 S_1 . D_1 S_1 . S_1 + D_2 S_1 . S_1 . D_1 S_1 + S_1 . D_2 S_1 . D_1 S_1 \\
&\quad + D_1 S_1 . D_2 S_1 . S_1 + D_1 S_1 . S_1 . D_2 S_1 + S_1 . D_1 S_1 . D_2 S_1 \\
&\quad + D_1 S_1 . D_1 S_1 . D_1 S_1 \\
&= 10 S_1^3,
\end{aligned}$$

and this coefficient of S_1^3 arises because the number of compositions of the number 3 into 3 parts is 10.

This example establishes that the effect of D_m upon $S_1^{k_1}$ is to multiply $S_1^{k_1}$ by a number equal to the number of compositions of m into k_1 parts, zero counting as a part. Hence by Art. 30

$$D_m S_1^{k_1} = \binom{m + k_1 - 1}{m} S_1^{k_1}.$$

67. The effect of D_m upon $S_2^{k_2}$ depends upon the compositions of m into k_2 even parts, zero taking its place as an even part. Hence unless m be even it causes $S_2^{k_2}$ to vanish. Considering then the symbol D_{2m} we observe that the compositions of $2m$ into even parts are equal in number to the whole number of compositions of m, for they are obtainable by multiplying by 2 each part of the latter composition.

Hence $\qquad\qquad\qquad D_{2m} S_2^{k_2} = \binom{m + k_2 - 1}{m} S_2^{k_2}.$

Generally there is no difficulty in establishing that

$$D_{im} S_i^{k_i} = \binom{m + k_i - 1}{m} S_i^{k_i}$$

while the result is zero if the suffix of the operative symbol is not a multiple of i.

68. Finally, consider the value of

$$D_m S_1^{k_1} S_2^{k_2} \dots S_i^{k_i}.$$

In dealing with the compositions of m into $k_1 + k_2 + \dots + k_i$ parts, zero counting as a part and retaining the factors of the operand in the above order, there is no condition that must be fulfilled by the first k_1 parts of the composition; the next k_2 parts must be multiples of 2; the next k_3 parts must be multiples of 3; ..., and finally, the last k_i parts must be multiples of i. Unless these conditions are satisfied the result of the operation derived from the composition will be zero. The complete result of the operation is the multiplication of the operand by an integer equal to the number of the compositions of m which have the properties above set forth. This integer is equal to the coefficient of x^m in the development of the algebraic product

$$(1 + x + x^2 + \dots)^{k_1} (1 + x^2 + x^4 + \dots)^{k_2} \dots (1 + x^i + x^{2i} + \dots)^{k_i},$$

because in the ordered multiplication an exponent of x can only be made up of

$$
\begin{array}{cccccc}
k_1 & \text{numbers each divisible by unity} \\
k_2 & \text{''} & \text{''} & \text{''} & \text{''} & 2 \\
k_3 & \text{''} & \text{''} & \text{''} & \text{''} & 3 \\
\vdots & & & & & \vdots \\
k_i & \text{''} & \text{''} & \text{''} & \text{''} & i
\end{array}
$$

Hence
$$D_m S_1^{k_1} S_2^{k_2} \dots S_i^{k_i}$$

$= $ coefficient of x^m in

$$(1-x)^{-k_1} (1-x^2)^{-k_2} \dots (1-x^i)^{-k_i} S_1^{k_1} S_2^{k_2} \dots S_i^{k_i}.$$

69. In the light of this result consider the enumeration of the distributions of objects of specification $(pqr\dots)$ into two or fewer similar boxes, or, what is the same question, the enumeration of the partitions of the multipartite number $(pqr\dots)$ into two or fewer parts. By Art. 62 we seek the coefficient of the function $(pqr\dots)$ in the development of

$$U_2 = \frac{1}{2!}(S_1^2 + S_2).$$

This is equal to the *first term in*

$$D_p D_q D_r \dots \frac{1}{2!}(S_1^2 + S_2),$$

which materialises when, after the operations, we put each of the quantities S_1, S_2 equal to unity.

Now by the theorem that has been established in Art. 65

$$D_{p_1} \frac{1}{2\,!}\,(S_1^2 + S_2)$$

is equal to the coefficient of $x_1^{p_1}$ in

$$\frac{1}{2}\left\{\frac{S_1^2}{(1-x_1)^2} + \frac{S_2}{1-x_1^2}\right\} \equiv \frac{1}{2}\frac{(S_1^2 + S_2) + x_1(S_1^2 - S_2)}{(1-x_1)(1-x_1^2)}\,.$$

Hence the coefficient of the function (p_1) is, putting $S_1 = S_2 = 1$, the coefficient of $x_1^{p_1}$ in

$$\frac{1}{(1-x_1)(1-x_1^2)}\,.$$

This number enumerates the partitions of the (unipartite) number p_1 into two or fewer parts and solves the corresponding problem in distributions.

This result is of course well known since the time of Euler.

70. Proceeding from the result

$$D_{p_1}\tfrac{1}{2}\,(S_1^2 + S_2) = \text{coeff. of } x_1^{p_1} \text{ in}$$

$$\frac{1}{2}\left\{\frac{S_1^2}{(1-x_1)^2} + \frac{S_2}{1-x_1^2}\right\}$$

we can further operate with the symbol D_{p_2} and find that

$$D_{p_1} D_{p_2}\tfrac{1}{2}\,(S_1^2 + S_2) = \text{coeff. of } x_1^{p_1}x_2^{p_2} \text{ in}$$

$$\frac{1}{2}\left\{\frac{S_1^2}{(1-x_1)^2(1-x_2)^2} + \frac{S_2}{(1-x_1^2)(1-x_2^2)}\right\},$$

shewing us that the coeff. of the function $(p_1 p_2)$ is equal to the coeff. of $x_1^{p_1}x_2^{p_2}$ in

$$\frac{1}{2}\left\{\frac{1}{(1-x_1)^2(1-x_2)^2} + \frac{1}{(1-x_1^2)(1-x_2^2)}\right\}$$

$$= \frac{1+x_1x_2}{(1-x_1)(1-x_1^2)\,.\,(1-x_2)(1-x_2^2)}\,.$$

This number enumerates the partitions of the bipartite number $(p_1 p_2)$ into two or fewer parts and solves the corresponding problem in distributions.

Further, if we denote by $P(pq, 2)$, $P(p, 2)$ the numbers of the partitions of (pq) and (p) into two or fewer parts we see that we may write

$$P(p_1 p_2, 2) = P(p_1, 2) P(p_2, 2) + P(p_1 - 1, 2) P(p_2 - 1, 2),$$

a convenient formula. As an example

$$P(33, 2) = \{P(3, 2)\}^2 + \{P(2, 2)\}^2,$$

and observing that the numbers 3, 2 have each of them 2 partitions into 2 or fewer parts

$$P(33, 2) = 2^2 + 2^2 = 8.$$

The 8 partitions, thus enumerated, are

$$(33), \quad (32, 01), \quad (23, 10), \quad (31, 02),$$
$$(13, 20), \quad (22, 11), \quad (21, 12), \quad (30, 03).$$

In general, since $P(2p, 2) = p + 1 = P(2p + 1, 2)$, we have the formulae

$$P(2p_1, 2p_2, 2) = (p_1 + 1)(p_2 + 1) + p_1 p_2,$$
$$P(2p_1, 2p_2 + 1, 2) = (2p_1 + 1)(p_2 + 1),$$
$$P(2p_1 + 1, 2p_2 + 1, 2) = 2(p_1 + 1)(p_2 + 1).$$

71. For the multipartite number $(p_1 p_2 \ldots p_s)$ we find that

$$D_{p_1} D_{p_2} \ldots D_{p_s} \tfrac{1}{2}(S_1^2 + S_2) = \text{coeff. of } x_1^{p_1} x_2^{p_2} \ldots x_s^{p_s} \text{ in}$$

$$\frac{1}{2} \left\{ \frac{S_1^2}{(1 - x_1)^2 (1 - x_2)^2 \ldots (1 - x_s)^2} + \frac{S_2}{(1 - x_1^2)(1 - x_2^2) \ldots (1 - x_s^2)} \right\},$$

and thence we establish that the partitions of the multipartite number $(p_1 p_2 \ldots p_s)$, into two or fewer parts, are enumerated by the coeff. of $x_1^{p_1} x_2^{p_2} \ldots x_s^{p_s}$ in

$$\frac{1}{2} \left\{ \frac{1}{(1 - x_1)^2 (1 - x_2)^2 \ldots (1 - x_s)^2} + \frac{1}{(1 - x_1^2)(1 - x_2^2) \ldots (1 - x_s^2)} \right\},$$

or in

$$\frac{1 + \Sigma x_1 x_2 + \Sigma x_1 x_2 x_3 x_4 + \ldots}{(1 - x_1)(1 - x_1^2) . (1 - x_2)(1 - x_2^2) \ldots (1 - x_s)(1 - x_s^2)},$$

the last numerator term being $\Sigma x_1 x_2 \ldots x_{s-1}$ or $\Sigma x_1 x_2 \ldots x_s$, according as s is uneven or even.

From this result general formulae may be constructed as above for the particular case $s = 2$.

72. Passing to the partitions into three or fewer parts we have
$$U_3 = \tfrac{1}{6}\left(S_1^3 + 3S_1 S_2 + 2S_3\right),$$
$D_{p_1} U_3$ equal to the coeff. of $x_1^{p_1}$ in
$$\frac{1}{6}\left\{\frac{S_1^3}{(1-x_1)^3} + 3\,\frac{S_1 S_2}{(1-x_1)(1-x_1^2)} + 2\,\frac{S_3}{1-x_1^3}\right\},$$
and thence the coeff. of the function (p_1) in U_3 is equal to the coeff. of $x_1^{p_1}$ in
$$\frac{1}{6}\left\{\frac{1}{(1-x_1)^3} + 3\,\frac{1}{(1-x_1)(1-x_1^2)} + 2\,\frac{1}{1-x_1^3}\right\},$$
or in
$$\frac{1}{(1-x_1)(1-x_1^2)(1-x_1^3)},$$
the well-known result in the case of the unipartite numbers.

Similarly for the partitions of bipartite numbers we are led to the coeff. of $x_1^{p_1}x_2^{p_2}$ in
$$\frac{1}{6}\left\{\frac{1}{(1-x_1)^3.(1-x_2)^3} + 3\,\frac{1}{(1-x_1)(1-x_1^2).(1-x_2)(1-x_2^2)}\right.$$
$$\left. + 2\,\frac{1}{(1-x_1^3).(1-x_2^3)}\right\},$$
or in
$$\frac{1 + x_1 x_2 + x_1^2 x_2 + x_1 x_2^2 + x_1^2 x_2^2 + x_1^3 x_2^3}{(1-x_1)(1-x_1^2)(1-x_1^3).(1-x_2)(1-x_2^2)(1-x_2^3)}.$$

73. In general for the case of the partitions of s-partite numbers into three or fewer parts we are led to the coeff. of $x_1^{p_1}x_2^{p_2}\ldots x_s^{p_s}$ in
$$\frac{1}{6}\left\{\frac{1}{(1-x_1)^3(1-x_2)^3\ldots(1-x_s)^3}\right.$$
$$+ 3\,\frac{1}{(1-x_1)(1-x_1^2).(1-x_2)(1-x_2^2)\ldots(1-x_s)(1-x_s^2)}$$
$$\left. + 2\,\frac{1}{(1-x_1^3)(1-x_2^3)\ldots(1-x_s^3)}\right\}.$$

In a similar manner the enumerating generating function for the partitions of the multipartite numbers $(p_1 p_2 \ldots p_s)$ into m or fewer parts can be constructed and the general problem of distribution before us may be regarded as solved.

74. For the partitions of the unipartite number p_1 into m or fewer parts the generating function comes out, after simplification, in the Eulerian form
$$\frac{1}{(1-x_1)(1-x_1^2)\ldots(1-x_1^m)}.$$

75. The final and most general case of distribution presents itself when the objects have the specification $(p_1 p_2 \ldots p_s)$ and the boxes the specification $(m_1 m_2 \ldots m_t)$, the whole number of the boxes being any number not greater than the whole number of the objects.

Here the enumerating generating function is

$$U_{m_1} U_{m_2} \ldots U_{m_t},$$

in which we seek the coeff. of the function

$$(p_1 p_2 \ldots p_s).$$

For consider any distribution of the objects into the boxes. It consists of objects having a certain specification distributed into boxes of specification (m_1), together with objects of other specifications distributed into boxes of specifications (m_2), (m_3), $\ldots (m_t)$ respectively. The aggregate of these specifications of combinations of objects constitutes a composition of the multipartite numbers $(p_1 p_2 \ldots p_s)$ into t or fewer parts, multipartite parts consisting wholly of zeros being admissible. Since any combination of objects may appertain to any set and the sets are not interchangeable, we obtain the generating function by simply multiplying together the generating functions which belong to the separate sets of boxes.

76. The application of this theorem to the distribution of objects of specification (p_1) is interesting. The enumerating function is

$$\frac{1}{(1-x)(1-x^2)\ldots(1-x^{m_1})}$$

$$\times \frac{1}{(1-x)(1-x^2)\ldots(1-x^{m_2})}$$

$$\times \frac{1}{(1-x)(1-x^2)\ldots(1-x^{m_3})}$$

$$\times \ldots\ldots\ldots\ldots\ldots\ldots\ldots\ldots$$

$$\times \frac{1}{(1-x)(1-x^2)\ldots(1-x^{m_t})}$$

$$\equiv \frac{1}{(1-x)^{n_1}(1-x^2)^{n_2}(1-x^3)^{n_3}\ldots},$$

where the succession of numbers $n_1, n_2, n_3, \ldots$ is related to the succession $m_1, m_2, m_3, \ldots m_t$ in the following manner.

We write down $m_1, m_2, m_3, \ldots m_t$ units in succession

$$\begin{array}{llllll} 1 & 1 & 1 & 1 & \ldots m_1 & \text{units} \\ 1 & 1 & 1 & 1 & \ldots m_2 & \text{,,} \\ 1 & 1 & 1 & 1 & \ldots m_3 & \text{,,} \\ \multicolumn{6}{c}{\ldots\ldots\ldots\ldots\ldots\ldots} \\ 1 & 1 & 1 & 1 & \ldots m_t & \text{,,} \end{array}$$

the numbers m_1, m_2, m_3 ... being assumed in descending order of magnitude and then add by columns producing a partition $(n_1, n_2, n_3, ...)$ which is said to be conjugate to $(m_1 m_2 ... m_t)$.

We have therefore a remarkable theorem :—

"The number of distributions of objects of specification (p) into boxes of specification $(m_1 m_2 ... m_t)$ is given by the coeff. of x^p in the function

$$(1 - x)^{-n_1} (1 - x^2)^{-n_2} (1 - x^3)^{-n_3} ...$$

where $(n_1 n_2 n_3 ...)$ is the partition conjugate to $(m_1 m_2 ... m_t)$."

77. As a verification observe that if $(m_1 m_2 ... m_t) \equiv (m)$ the conjugate partition is (1^m) and the enumerating function is

$$(1 - x)^{-1} (1 - x^2)^{-1} ... (1 - x^m)^{-1},$$

whereas if $(m_1 m_2 ... m_t) \equiv (1^m)$ the conjugate partition is (m) and the enumerating function is

$$(1 - x)^{-m}.$$

As another example suppose $(m_1 m_2 ... m_t) \equiv (221)$; the conjugate partition is (32) and the enumerating function is

$$(1 - x)^{-3} (1 - x^2)^{-2},$$

which is
$$1 + 3x + 8x^2 + 16x^3 + 30x^4 + ...$$

The distributions of the assemblages a^2, a^3 are

A	A	B	B	C
a^2	•	•	•	•
•	•	a^2	•	•
•	•	•	•	a^2
a	a	•	•	•
a	•	a	•	•
a	•	•	•	a
•	•	a	a	•
•	•	a	•	a

No. = 8

A	A	B	B	C
a^3	•	•	•	•
•	•	a^3	•	•
•	•	•	•	a^3
a^2	a	•	•	•
a^2	•	a	•	•
a^2	•	•	•	a
•	•	a^2	a	•
•	•	a^2	•	a
a	•	a^2	•	•
a	•	•	•	a^2
•	•	a	•	a^2
a	a	a	•	•
a	a	•	•	a
a	•	a	a	•
a	•	a	•	a
•	•	a	a	a

No. = 16

78. If we restrict the symmetric functions utilised so that no part greater than k appears the effect is to restrict the distributions to the extent that not more than k similar objects can appear in any one box.

We may usefully examine the case $k = 1$.

Instead of the functions S_1, S_2, ... we take

$$A_1 = 1 + (1) + (1^2) + (1^3) + \dots,$$
$$A_2 = 1 + (2) + (2^2) + (2^3) + \dots,$$
$$\dotfill$$
$$A_m = 1 + (m) + (m^2) + (m^3) + \dots;$$

and then
$$U_1 = A_1,$$
$$2!\, U_2 = A_1^2 + A_2,$$
$$3!\, U_3 = A_1^3 + 3A_1 A_2 + 2A_3,$$
$$\dotfill$$

$$m!\, U_m = \Sigma \frac{m!}{m_1!\, m_2!\, m_3! \dots} \left(\frac{A_1}{1}\right)^{m_1} \left(\frac{A_2}{2}\right)^{m_2} \left(\frac{A_3}{3}\right)^{m_3} \dots.$$

79. For the operation of the D symbol we have
$$D_1 A_1 = A_1,\ D_0 A_1 = A_1,\ D_m A_1 = 0 \text{ in other cases,}$$

and generally
$$D_s A_m = A_m \text{ when } s = m \text{ or zero,}$$
$$D_s A_m = 0 \text{ in every other case.}$$

Also the symbol, operating through the composition of its suffix into units, yields

$$D_k A_1^m = \binom{m}{k} A_1^m; \quad D_{sk} A_s^m = \binom{m}{k} A_s^m.$$

For the operand
$$A_1^{m_1} A_2^{m_2} \dots A_i^{m_i}$$

the symbol D_s operates through the compositions of s into

$$m_1 + m_2 + \dots + m_i \text{ parts,}$$

zero counting as a part. From the law of operation given above it can be seen that for the operation associated with such a composition to have an effect other than zero,

the first m_1 parts must be zero or unity,

next m_2	,,	,,	two
,, m_3	,,	,,	three
$\vdots$ $\vdots$			$\vdots$
,, m_i	,,	,,	i

The number of such compositions is the coefficient of x^s in the product

$$(1+x)^{m_1}(1+x^2)^{m_2}(1+x^3)^{m_3}\ldots(1+x^i)^{m_i}$$

as is evident when the orderly multiplication is carried out (cf. Art. 14). Thence

$$D_s A_1{}^{m_1} A_2{}^{m_2} \ldots A_i{}^{m_i}$$

$$= A_1{}^{m_1} A_2{}^{m_2} \ldots A_i{}^{m_i} \times \text{coefficient of } x^s \text{ in } (1+x)^{m_1}(1+x^2)^{m_2}\ldots(1+x^i)^{m_i} *.$$

80. To apply this result, consider the distributing of objects of specification $(2^{k_2}1^{k_1})$ into two or fewer similar boxes—in other words, the partitions of the multipartite number $(2^{k_2}1^{k_1})$ into two or fewer parts subject to the restriction that no box is to contain two similar objects—or no constituent of the multipartite parts to involve numbers greater than unity.

We find that

$$D_2 U_2 = D_2\left(\tfrac{1}{2}A_1{}^2 + \tfrac{1}{2}A_2\right) = \tfrac{1}{2}A_1{}^2 + \tfrac{1}{2}A_2,$$

because the coefficients of x^2 in $(1+x)^2$ and in $(1+x^2)$ are both unity. Hence

$$D_2{}^{k_2} U_2 = \tfrac{1}{2}A_1{}^2 + \tfrac{1}{2}A_2.$$

Now $$D_1 U_2 = D_1\left(\tfrac{1}{2}A_1{}^2 + \tfrac{1}{2}A_2\right) = A_1{}^2,$$

because the coefficients of x in $(1+x)^2$ and in $(1+x^2)$ are 2 and zero respectively.

Hence by repeated operation

$$D_2{}^{k_2} D_1{}^{k_1} U_2 = 2^{k_1-1} A_1{}^2,$$

establishing that the coefficient of the function $(2^{k_2}1^{k_1})$ in U_2 is

$$2^{k_1-1}.$$

Ex. gr. Suppose that the objects for distribution are

$$a\ a\ \beta\ \beta\ \gamma\ \gamma\ \delta\ \epsilon\ \theta,$$

so that $$k_2 = k_1 = 3.$$

The distributions—four in number—are

A	A
$a\beta\gamma\delta\epsilon\theta$	$a\beta\gamma$
$a\beta\gamma\delta\epsilon$	$a\beta\gamma\theta$
$a\beta\gamma\delta\theta$	$a\beta\gamma\epsilon$
$a\beta\gamma\epsilon\theta$	$a\beta\gamma\delta$

---

* The reader will observe that when the magnitude of the parts of the partitions is restricted to be not greater than the integer k, the corresponding function of x is

$$(1+x+x^2+\ldots+x^k)^{m_1}(1+x^2+x^4+\ldots+x^{2k})^{m_2}\ldots(1+x^i+x^{2i}+\ldots+x^{ki})^{m_i}$$

$$\equiv \left(\frac{1-x^{k+1}}{1-x}\right)^{m_1}\left(\frac{1-x^{2k+2}}{1-x^2}\right)^{m_2}\ldots\left(\frac{1-x^{ik+i}}{1-x^i}\right)^{m_i}.$$

Again, let the objects be of specification $(3^{k_3}2^{k_2}1^{k_1})$ and let there be three or fewer similar boxes, the distributions being subject to the same restriction as before.

We find that

$$D_3\tfrac{1}{6}(A_1^3 + 3A_1A_2 + 2A_3) = \tfrac{1}{6}(A_1^3 + 3A_1A_2 + 2A_3),$$

because the coefficients of x^3 in

$$(1+x)^3,\ (1+x)(1+x^2),\ (1+x^3)$$

are all equal to unity.

Hence $\qquad D_3^{k_3}$ gives $\tfrac{1}{6}(A_1^3 + 3A_1A_2 + 2A_3)$.

Now the coefficients of x^2 in the three functions of x are 3, 1 and 0.

Hence $\qquad D_2\tfrac{1}{6}(A_1^3 + 3A_1A_2 + 2A_3) = \tfrac{1}{2}(A_1^3 + A_1A_2)$

and $\qquad D_3^{k_3}D_2^{k_2}\tfrac{1}{6}(A_1^3 + 3A_1A_2 + 2A_3) = \tfrac{1}{2}(3^{k_2-1}A_1^3 + A_1A_2),$

and finally

$$D_3^{k_3}D_2^{k_2}D_1^{k_1}\tfrac{1}{6}(A_1^3 + 3A_1A_2 + 2A_3) = \tfrac{1}{2}(3^{k_2+k_1-1}A_1^3 + A_1A_2),$$

establishiug that the coefficient of the function $(3^{k_3}2^{k_2}1^{k_1})$ in U_3 is

$$\tfrac{1}{2}(3^{k_2+k_1-1} + 1).$$

Ex. gr. If the objects to be distributed are

$$aaa\ \ \beta\beta\beta\ \ \gamma\gamma\ \ \delta\delta\ \ \epsilon\epsilon\ \ \theta,$$

so that $\qquad k_3 = 2,\ \ k_2 = 3,\ \ k_1 = 1$

we have the fourteen distributions

A	A	A	A	A	A
$a\beta\gamma\delta\epsilon\theta$	$a\beta\gamma\delta\epsilon$	$a\beta$	$a\beta\gamma\delta\epsilon$	$a\beta\gamma\delta\epsilon$	$a\beta\theta$
$a\beta\gamma\delta\epsilon\theta$	$a\beta\delta\epsilon$	$a\beta\gamma$	$a\beta\gamma\epsilon\theta$	$a\beta\delta\epsilon$	$a\beta\gamma\delta$
$a\beta\gamma\delta\epsilon\theta$	$a\beta\gamma\epsilon$	$a\beta\delta$	$a\beta\gamma\delta\epsilon$	$a\beta\delta\theta$	$a\beta\gamma\epsilon$
$a\beta\gamma\delta\epsilon\theta$	$a\beta\gamma\delta$	$a\beta\epsilon$	$a\beta\gamma\delta\epsilon$	$a\beta\delta\epsilon$	$a\beta\gamma\theta$
$a\beta\gamma\delta\epsilon$	$a\beta\delta\epsilon\theta$	$a\beta\gamma$	$a\beta\delta\epsilon\theta$	$a\beta\gamma\delta$	$a\beta\gamma\epsilon$
$a\beta\gamma\epsilon\theta$	$a\beta\gamma\delta\epsilon$	$a\beta\delta$	$a\beta\gamma\delta\theta$	$a\beta\gamma\epsilon$	$a\beta\delta\epsilon$
$a\beta\gamma\delta\epsilon$	$a\beta\gamma\delta\theta$	$a\beta\epsilon$	$a\beta\gamma\delta\epsilon$	$a\beta\gamma\delta$	$a\beta\epsilon\theta$

81. In general to shew the nature of the theorems more clearly we observe that

$$D_{p_1}D_{p_2}\dots D_{p_s}U_2 = \text{coefficient of } x_1^{p_1}x_2^{p_2}\dots x_s^{p_s} \text{ in}$$
$$\tfrac{1}{2}\{(1+x_1)(1+x_2)\dots(1+x_s)\}^2 A_1^2$$
$$+ \tfrac{1}{2}(1+x_1^2)(1+x_2^2)\dots(1+x_s^2)A_2,$$

so that the enumerating function is

$$\tfrac{1}{2}\{(1+x_1)(1+x_2)\ldots(1+x_s)\}^2$$
$$+\tfrac{1}{2}(1+x_1^2)(1+x_2^2)\ldots(1+x_s^2),$$

and similarly, derived from

$$D_{p_1}D_{p_2}\ldots D_{p_s}U_3,$$

we obtain the enumerating function

$$\tfrac{1}{6}\{(1+x_1)(1+x_2)\ldots(1+x_s)\}^3$$
$$+\tfrac{1}{2}\{(1+x_1)(1+x_2)\ldots(1+x_s)$$
$$\times(1+x_1^2)(1+x_2^2)\ldots(1+x_s^2)\}$$
$$+\tfrac{1}{3}(1+x_1^3)(1+x_2^3)\ldots(1+x_s^3),$$

and so on in the higher cases.

In conclusion it will be clear that an important part of the Theory of Combinations and Permutations is intimately connected with the Theory of Symmetric Functions in elementary algebra.

In Combinatory Analysis, by the author, the correspondence is carried much further and it is shewn that either theory is a powerful instrument of research in the other. The fact is that in theorems of Combinations and Permutations the entities dealt with come into consideration in a symmetrical manner and a symmetrical method of investigation is at once suggested. Moreover it will be found in nearly every case that the appropriate method, though it may be in appearance devoid of symmetry, is when sufficiently examined, symmetrical. The binomial coefficients which enter largely into combinatory theorems are themselves symmetric functions of zero weight. Ex. gr.

$$\Sigma a^0 \quad = (0) = \binom{n}{1}$$

$$\Sigma a^0\beta^0 \quad = (0^2) = \binom{n}{2}$$

$$\Sigma a^0\beta^0\gamma^0 = (0^3) = \binom{n}{3}$$

$$\vdots$$

the number of the quantities a, β, γ, ... being n.

There is an algebra of these numerical functions which deals with their representation by means of partitions with zero parts and we find an appropriate operator

$$D_0$$

which operates through the compositions of zero into zero parts. These are identical with the partitions of zero into zero parts and are infinite in number, viz. :—

$$0, 00, 000, 0000, \ldots\ldots \text{ ad inf.}$$

It has been noted that the operator

$$D_m$$

where m is a positive integer > 0 is in fact a partial differential operator of the order m. When $m = 0$, we find that the operator is one that is met with in the Calculus of Finite Differences.

There is throughout a corresponding theory of the enumeration of numbered diagrams of the 'Magic Square' type which has been much developed and will without doubt be the subject {of further investigations.

www.ingramcontent.com/pod-product-compliance
Lightning Source LLC
Chambersburg PA
CBHW072113150726
47999CB00005B/2012